Terry-Thomas Tells Tales

Terry-Thomas
Tells Tales

An Autobiography

Terry-Thomas with Terry Daum

 Robson Books

This book is dedicated to the memory of
Lady (Isobel) Barnett
who gave much more than she took.

First published in Great Britain in 1990 by
Robson Books Ltd,
Bolsover House, 5-6 Clipstone Street,
London W1P 7EB

This Robson paperback edition
first published in 1992

British Library Cataloguing-in-Publication Data
A catalogue record for this book is available
from the British Library

ISBN 0 86051 795 0

Printed in Hungary

Contents

Acknowledgements

A number of people contributed to the production of this book by providing help, support, suggestions and information over the years.

For assistance in Majorca, I should like to thank Belinda Terry-Thomas for her kindness, co-operation and cooking! Also Joan Tow, Sue (Kaufman) Shiers, Gabrielle Stock, Unity Grantham, Shelagh McAlpine de Rubio, Joan Sherwood, Olga and Robert Jaras, Richard Headridge and Felix Celis Torras.

In Ibiza, thanks to: Patsy Dodd, Nina van Pallandt, Edith Sommer Maloney, Susie and Denholm Elliott, Ted Falcon-Barker, Sandy Pratt (and not forgetting three helpful island characters who have passed on: Mimi Reynolds, Viscount Maugham and Elmyr de Hory).

In Britain, my thanks to: Sir Harry Secombe, Jack Douglas, Margaret and Cliff Pearson, Rachel Martin and the *Daily Telegraph* and *Evening Standard* for kindly giving me access to their cuttings libraries.

Terry Daum

Foreword by Jack Douglas

True characters in the world of show business are very few and far between, therefore my memory of the first time I saw Terry-Thomas is remarkably strong. He was appearing in *Piccadilly Hayride* with another famous comedian, Sid Field, at the Prince of Wales Theatre in London during the war, and I was so impressed that I made a note in my diary: 'saw a great, promising star last night called Terry-Thomas'. So it was with great pride that I watched his career going from strength to strength and, before his dreadful illness struck him down, he became one of the few truly international stars.

On and off stage or screen he was always Terry-Thomas. Long may his memory live.

Jack Douglas

1   How I Escaped from Finchley

I've been called any number of things in print. T-T with his permanent air of caddish disdain ... bounder ... aristocratic rogue ... upper-class English twit ... genuine English eccentric ... one of the last real gentlemen ... wet, genteel Englishman ... high-bred idiot ... cheeky blighter ... camel-haired cad ... amiable buffoon ... pompous Englishman ... twentieth-century dandy ... stinker ... king of the cads ...

All those descriptions added up to my public image as Terry-Thomas.

Initially, my attitude to acting had never been to play myself but another character. I changed my opinion when I found that people just wanted me to play the classic Terry-Thomas character which I had developed in real life. It seemed remarkable that that was all I had to do in film after film. I was never a trophy hunter so it didn't worry me that the character I had become brought no awards. Once I had cornered the market, in the Sixties, as Hollywood's favourite silly-ass Englishman, the work piled up. It didn't bother me one bit that I had become type-cast. Perhaps it should have concerned me more. I was stereotyped but then – I didn't fancy myself as a nun!

Since my early days as a clerk with a cold storage company at Smithfield Market when I wore a double-breasted suit with a carnation and suede shoes, I could see how absurd the character was and the comic possibilities began to dawn on me. Generally speaking, people have always regarded me as being the classic Englishman-about-town. But if you had suggested that to Robert Morley, Wilfrid Hyde White or David Niven, they would probably have said a very old English word indeed. Because – while they were all real English *gentlemen*, I wasn't! I was always more cosmopolitan; some kind of nut. It was just my good luck that I was able to earn a great deal of money by sending up pompous Englishmen, the sort of people to whom I had been exposed a lot as a young man. But I wasn't one of them. I suppose really I've cashed in on playing the lower-middle-class pretending to be upper-class.

Actually, how such an immaculate character as Terry-Thomas can have emanated from Finchley is something I shall never be able to answer. I'm sure few people have thought about Finchley in-depth (except, I suppose, Margaret Thatcher, whose constituency it is.) It certainly curdles my blood to think of that part of London where I was born, on 14 July 1911, in a house called Glenfern, in Nether Street.

I found the people and the area quite extraordinarily rough for even as a nipper I was a snob and I soon grew up to hate the place. Having as much style and originality as I thought I had, I knew I didn't fit into that part of the world. My own family were graced with very little style, indeed, they were positively coarse.

My father, Ernest Frederick Stevens, whose parents were jolly well-off and lived in Shepherd's Hill, then considered to be the nicest street in Highgate, was a stylish person up to a point. But, like my three brothers, John, Richard and William, he had the flat, toneless, London accent with very little character which I found so uninspiring.

On the other hand, my mother, Ellen Elizabeth Hoar, tried to speak like a duchess. A well-behaved duchess. And my only sister, Mary, was carefully brought-up to have excellent manners and exaggeratedly genteel accent. She still has both.

Try as I did, I, Thomas Terry Hoar Stevens, never felt part of that family. I could never fathom out what they were supposed to be. How strange it was, I used to ponder, that I'd got such a peculiar background.

It annoyed me terribly that I should ever have to introduce some of my relations to my friends. Except for my mother and sister, I was ashamed of the lot of them.

My mother had been one of twelve children who had all gone to different schools and subsequently spoke with various nondescript accents. None of them had the accent I was looking for – posh! Yes, that's it, posh! Years later one of my aunts asked me, 'Tom, why do you have such a peculiar way of talking?' That intrigued me because I thought that *she* had.

My father was a sportive, extrovert person who had done a bit of dancing and singing in amateur theatricals. I remember, when I was about four, standing in the road watching fascinated as a long, upright piano he had bought was delivered and lifted inside. And a few years later, we got a wireless, a huge one with lots of knobs and a big loudspeaker which had to be tuned with a cat's whisker. We all used to gather round in the drawing-room to listen to the broadcasts – usually pretty poor stuff. I remember leaning up against a glass-fronted cabinet, filled with ornaments from Hong Kong and Bangkok and listening to songs like 'Love Sends its Little Gift of Roses'.

Thinking back, I'm sure we only had a wireless (which was rare in those days) because my father had been in a mellow mood and bought it while he was sloshed. He liked getting sloshed. While he was exclusively a whisky-and-soda man, my mother did not specialize. She drank anything. Regularly. But I never once saw her anywhere near intoxicated. Well-behaved duchesses naturally took great care never to be seen to be tiddly.

Every summer we went in a hired limousine to spend two

months' holiday in a rented house at Combe Martin, Devon. It was always a bit of a puzzle to me why my father never joined us. Yet it never occurred to me to ask because, from a young age, I knew that my parents did not get on well together. With the years, they drifted further and further apart. Eventually they divorced and my father remarried.

I don't recall joining in my brothers' games or ever going out with them, though I suppose I must have done. While they liked to do things together I tended to be a loner. Or perhaps I just hated listening to their ill-formed vowels.

Of course there was a general feeling of disappointment when I was born. Another boy. The whole family had waited eagerly and patiently for a girl. My mother and father had done their nut trying for one. After giving birth to three lusty sons, my mother had just longed for a daughter. Then I came along! My theory is that the gap between my front teeth was caused by prenatal influence. When my sister was born, three-and-a-half years later, she had exactly the same gap.

One of my earliest recollections is of standing in the window of my mother's bedroom watching the baby being weighed on shiny new scales, by a nurse. She was carroty-red and smelt (not the baby, the nurse.) Clumsily she placed my little sister on the varnished, basket-weave cradle of the scales. I wonder why this made such an impression. Was I waiting to see if she would ever drop the baby? Was my banana-skin humour beginning to emerge?

This was the period that started real trouble for me because up to then I had been pampered by my mother. I had had a nap with her every afternoon before Mary arrived, and I loved it. Suddenly, I had to get used to waking up with an emptiness all around me in place of my mother's voluptuous form. It was there, in the warm security of her bed where, precociously, my love of female bosoms began.

So I was very, very put out at being swept to one side by Mary, for all the attention had been mine up to then. She was so adored and cherished by everybody that jealousy could easily have turned me against her, but I didn't resent her. What I resented was the injustice of a situation where I was no longer 'the baby'.

To keep in the picture and compensate for this displacement, I started pulling funny faces – and have been doing it ever since. Most children use tears to get attention. I went for the laughs. I began 'entertaining' family visitors in the drawing-room by dressing up. Relentlessly I entertained anyone I could get to watch. I used to recite William Makepeace Thackeray's 'Little Billee', played heavily for laughs – which I always got. The poem finished, 'Down he fell on his bended knee' and I suited my action to the words. I also sang songs with a broad Devonshire burr and even devised my own ballet, 'The Dance of the Window Cleaner', using a basin and filthy wet rag as props.

As you can see, there was no end to my inventiveness!

When I was about ten, my mother, no longer able to ignore my Thespian leanings, started taking me to the theatre. We trotted off to the Golders Green Hippodrome (later, when I had 'made it' I often topped the bill there), or caught a tram to the West End and went to shows at the London Hippodrome or the Coliseum. By now I had been taken out of my habitual sailor suits and put into dark clothes. I adored this. Very smart and grown-up I felt as I sat in the stalls beside mother and watched productions like Somerset Maugham's 'The Letter.'

It was during this time that I discovered Owen Nares. I can't recall in which play I first saw him perform, but his beautifully modulated voice made a lasting impression on me. I thought his voice was perfection – what good diction was all about. It was hearing Owen Nares's delivery that indelibly impressed on me the importance of developing a good style of English. I determined to speak grammatically at all times and use an interesting and extensive vocabulary. Inherently I realized that good speech automatically suggested that you were well-educated and made people look up to you.

I got my first glimpse of Hollywood when Mother began

taking us to the Bohemia cinema at Church End, Finchley, and to the Odeon, Golders Green. (That Odeon is still my favourite cinema. I've always adored it. I just wish I'd bought it for myself years ago!)

Up on the screen we met the great names of Hollywood: Douglas Fairbanks Snr, Mary Pickford, Charlie Chaplin, Fatty Arbuckle, Buster Keaton, Gloria Swanson ...

If a fortune teller had told me then that years later I would be standing in line at a Royal Command Performance in Cardiff, next to Gloria Swanson, I would have told her she was bonkers.

After attending various prep schools in Finchley, I was sent at thirteen to Ardingly College, Sussex. It was a bit more showy than my previous schools even though, somewhat to my disappointment, the other pupils did not have particularly posh accents. There were no Owen Nareses. There *was* a master named Major Plum-Crawford who spoke English with a really wild accent. One of his beauties was, 'Boy, go and get your garse masque (gas mask).'

Although school-life was more ceremonious than I'd been used to, I was stimulated by the change. The beautiful surroundings and the mellowed school buildings pleased me, especially the elegant chapel and bellows-pumped organ. Once I'd settled in, I started skylarking around to attract attention. I would do anything to attract attention. The satisfaction I got when I made people laugh was indescribably potent. I formed a jazz band which was named the Rhythm Maniacs, consisting of ukelele (played by me), piano and banjo. We played for school functions in a large hall called The Under where I soon became known as 'the funny chap with the gift of the gap'.

All the time we were playing, I used to dash around the platform doing what might be described as dancing. The chaps loved it, but I became unpopular with the staff after I had conducted the national anthem to a syncopated tempo while pulling faces. The head was peeved. He considered it very bad taste.

I was more of a duffer than a good pupil at Ardingly. As I was first only in carpentry and English, I never came near to being the intellectual to which I aspired, and this upset me more and more the older I grew. I was convinced that intellectualism must give one a tremendous feeling of power. But so did applause – another reason to go for the laughs.

The only scholarly thing I did that meant anything was coming top of the school in an Officers' Training Corps exam, the Certificate A. For a not-very-brilliant chap, I did jolly well. I found it easy because the subject dazzled me. Officers and gentlemen! After all, you had to learn how to be a gentleman before you could become a cad.

Whereas my virginity was eventually lost with the enthusiastic assistance of my father's housekeeper, my teenage sexual appetite was partially appeased with the help of a girl who had a double-barrelled name (of course!).

Barbara Vernon-Smith was one of my regular dancing partners whom I regarded as my steady girl-friend. She frequently entertained me in her bed-sitting-room although she was inhibited when it came to our actually going to bed together, possibly because her mother was downstairs. But she was fun and knew how to satisfy.

Her mother advised her once: 'Barbara. You really ought to take your bangles off when Tom comes to see you. They broadcast all your movements. I can tell exactly what you are doing up there.'

Miss Dixon came to housekeep for us when she was about twenty-two. I was a few years younger.

She was pleasant with a charming smile, dark-black hair (that's black plus) and a very smooth Cornish skin. She was the most masterful person. Or should I say mistressful? She became deeply interested in me. Hooked on me, in fact. And it wasn't long before she hooked me!

Our heady friendship went on for about a year. Many were the nights I was in her room when we heard my sister Mary moving about and I dived under the bed just in case she should come in and disturb Miss Dixon demonstrating one of her Cornish capers.

I was nearly seventeen when I left school and joined my father in Smithfield Market as a fifteen-shillings-a-week transport clerk with the Union Cold Storage Company. What I had done to deserve such a fate baffles me. However, I soon settled down and joined the firm's amateur dramatic society. I became one of their keenest members. When I made my début as the peppery Lord Trench in *The Dover Road*, I got as much kick out of this as if I had been elevated to the peerage. The buffoon in me was released so I had no difficulty with the acting. Let's face it – as I had to every morning when shaving – I had a naturally funny expression. If it couldn't launch a thousand ships at least it always launched the laughs. On stage, I knew automatically how to perform and because of my funny bone, I was able to get laughs at a twitch of a nostril.

I adopted an exaggerated style of dressing, an infallible way of attracting attention in England. It certainly attracted the attention of the managing director. One day he sent for me and made it plain he did not think that buttonholes and long cigarette holders were fitting for a singularly inexperienced junior clerk.

'You look more like a juvenile lead in a musical comedy,' he said with distaste. 'Oh, how awful!' I said, a frown masking my smug smile.

So, I was hopeless as a clerk, but who cared? At making the chaps chuckle I was a great success. I never stopped farting around.

I used to do the Hunchback of Notre Dame at the drop of a hat. Suddenly, I would leap up a pillar and make hideous faces, like Lon Chaney. Everyone loved it. Certainly nobody ever threw a side of beef at me. Come to think of it, someone did chuck a book. I caught it. It was *No Orchids for Miss Blandish* and I can highly recommend it.

In Smithfield Market I was known as 'the man with carpet slippers' because, like Sir Gerald du Maurier, I wore revolutionary suede shoes. We were probably the only two men in London who did. I wore mine because I had an injured foot from ice skating. I don't know why Sir Gerald wore his; I never asked him. Come to think of it, I never met him.

At eighteen, I had my first engagement as a paid entertainer. My fifteen-bob wages were not going very far so I fixed a booking at a social evening of the Union of Electric Railwaymen's Dining Club, at South Kensington, for thirty bob. But Thos Stevens, as I appeared in the programme, was not as funny as he thought he was. Not an overnight star, a flop, in fact! It had been precocious of me to attempt to make those boozy UER members laugh. You needed a good act and bags of experience for that sort of work. I repaired my damaged ego by making a couple of brief appearances in a Gilbert and Sullivan operetta with the Edgware Operatic Society.

Although I stayed in Smithfield for about six years, I never got the hang of the job. Fortunately, my chief was the producer of the plays we put on. He told me, one day, that he really ought to sack me for incompetence. But he could not afford to lose me from his cast.

By the time I was twenty-two, I had already decided that Smithfield was not the place for me. Just at the same time Smithfield decided likewise. I was suddenly booted out. I was delighted because they gave me a golden handshake – well, hardly golden – and I got a job from a friend of my brother, in an electrical store.

I posed as an electrical engineer. 'Oh yes, I'm experienced,' I said. Indeed, I had actually picked up over the years quite a few useful tips like how best to change electric light bulbs and peel fuse wire. This small knowledge, I quickly found out, hardly equipped me to be an electrical engineer. So I changed jobs. This time I was a door-to-door salesman trying to push electrical installations for the wiring of those houses that were, up to then, still lit by gas. Not too successfully. I didn't exactly leave a trail of brilliantly illuminated houses in my wake. One customer, however, was impressed enough to say to the electrician who went to fix the installations I had sold her: 'Your salesman is quite a card, isn't he? He even sang songs at the piano for me, played down at the bottom end, too. Just like a professional he was!'

Then there was my insurance-agent period, brief though it was, when I knocked on doors and brightly introduced myself as the agent for the Norwich Union. But my heart wasn't in it. Not one policy was bought. Terrible feeling not selling anything. I had let the company down and gave in my notice after about a week.

There were lots more dabbles in lots more professions. Every dabble seemed to prove that the only thing I was good at was attracting people's attention and making them laugh.

I cultivated my aptitude for dancing by giving exhibitions, sometimes partnered by none less than Jessie Matthews's sister. And every Wednesday I went to Dickins and Jones's tea dances with a girl called Kay Shires. Kay and I twirled sedately round and round while her mother ate countless cream pastries. It would have been polite to offer Mrs Shires a dance, but she was always too busy eating cakes.

I also helped with the classes at Aida Foster's School of Dancing, Golders Green. And for a time I was a professional ballroom dancer at the Cricklewood Palais de Danse, but fortunately, I wasn't dedicated enough, otherwise – who knows? – I might have become a gigolo.

In my mid twenties I was able to leave Finchley behind me (good ho!) and move in with John Barnes, a friend of mine who had a delightful mews flat overlooking Lord's cricket ground: one room, kitchen and bathroom for thirty bob a week.

John was a cough-drop, a bit of a card. He dressed immaculately with bowler hat and brolly, had a Velázquez moustache and an Oxford accent that you could cut with a knife.

His appearance perfectly complemented my own which, at this period, comprised an Anthony Eden homburg, black coat, hounds-tooth trousers, pearl-grey waistcoat and the clove carnation without which I never ventured abroad. Nor, for that matter, on a number thirteen bus.

John and I shared his flat for a couple of years and spent a lot of time together until he moved to another place that was cheaper. As he so rarely paid anything towards the rent anyway, the move seemed to me to be rather unnecessary.

John earned his living as a film extra. He did quite well out it. Extras were paid one guinea for a day's work and thirty bob if required to wear tails or a dinner-jacket; what was described as a dress-call. On top of the basic fee, they were given an extra something which could range from thirty bob to five quid.

One day, I stood in for John. He was going away for a long weekend and he suggested that I might like to go down to Pinewood.

'Why don't you go and present yourself?' he said. 'You will have a bit of fun and pick yourself up some lolly. Here, take my card, you'll need it to get in.'

So I did and immediately realized that this work suited me down to the ground. It wasn't really like work to me. I got an enormous kick out of it: playing poker, drinking champagne-and-Guinness for elevenses and telling the crowd funny stories during the long waits between takes.

After that, John and I often went to the studios together. It was fascinating because one never knew what one might pick up.

One day I was chosen to dance with the star of the film, Jean Colin. I was thrilled. I was probably chosen only for my height – six foot – but I was thrilled anyway.

It was all beginning to happen.

In Vic Oliver's *Rhythm in the Air* (1937) I played 'someone who looks like a cad and a drunk and can tap-dance'. The same year, in Jack Buchanan's *This'll Make You Whistle* I had to dive into a tank of water at Elstree – and suffered from impaired hearing for years afterwards. (This condition was to get me down-graded in the Army, putting paid to my hopes of getting a commission.) In *Climbing*

High, one of Jessie Matthews' films, I was heard but not seen. I was paid a fiver to moo like a cow, having spread it around that I could do animal noises. It was said that I gave a most sensitive, impeccable performance.

Several times I was actually picked to talk. Not many words, mind. Not what one could describe as having a speaking role, but better than the extras who were never heard at all. I once advertised myself in Variety as 'Terry-Thomas, the man who said, "A Thousand!" in "Once in a Million."' All I had had to do was shout out, 'A Thousand!' in an auction scene.

Yes — by now I had become Terry-Thomas. Tom Stevens was not suitable as a stage name and I considered various possibilities. I quite liked the sound of Thomas Terry but I decided I had to kill that one fast. I didn't want people to think I was trying to cash in on Ellen Terry's name and fame. So I turned my christian names round and added a hyphen for an individual touch.

Michael Wilding, Richard Greene and Stewart Granger were all fellow extras who appeared in the crowd scenes of film after film. One thing amazed me about those chaps. Without any difficulty, it seemed, they became stars and I was left out. Not until some years afterwards could I accept that despite all my impeccable turn-out, my face rather lacked that necessary allure. It was not that I was exactly expecting to become a glamorous film-star overnight, but it did seem a little bit unreasonable. My mother had always said I was so ugly that nobody would ever marry me — enough to make anyone grit the gap in their teeth!

After John moved out of the St John's Wood flat, a succession of jolly eager girls moved in — some for a night or two, some for longer. Most of them were extras I had met in the studios. Not one of them seemed to notice that the flat was decidedly dilapidated. My divan bed, for instance, was broken in the middle, held together by some complicated system of lashing splinters of wood and a car jack to the bed frame. From the amount of heavy work that the bed had to put up with, it was amazing there was anything left at all. Despite these numerous female visitors I did all my own housework. This didn't present any difficulty as I really enjoyed cooking, starching my collars and mending and would allow no one to help me.

Many years later, when I played the title role in *Lord Arthur Saville's Crime*, on television, I was enthralled to see that Ernest Thesiger, who was also in the cast, busied himself with weaving, between takes.

The skinny, gaunt-looking actor was a dab hand with his needle: embroidery, needle-point, tatting, he adored it all. In his Army days, an officer on his rounds one night realized that Pte Thesiger was not present.

'No sir,' he was told, 'You'll find him outside by a bush doing his needlework.'

The officer went out to investigate and there was Thesiger flashing away with his needle in just the same way he had done on the occasions he had been invited to join Queen Mary's sewing circle.

The year 1938 was memorable for two principal reasons. I did my first-ever impersonation in public and I made my first radio broadcast.

In the Little Grafton Theatre, Tottenham Court Road, I gave an inspired impression of George Formby and learned a lesson that was to be useful whenever I attempted impersonations. That first time, I accompanied myself on a Formby banjolele which had a picture of him on it. Looking at this picture made my mouth – and the other bits of me – adopt the right position at once. Like the other performers at that show at the Little Grafton, I was on a shares basis and was lucky to earn twenty-five shillings.

On Whit Monday I broadcast on the tea dance programme *Friends to Tea*. I didn't give a very good performance, largely because the producer, Ernest Longstaffe (someone I was never to get on with) wanted me to copy the shaggy-dog style of a delightful radio raconteur, A J Alan. It was never a good idea to copy anybody and I was a dismal failure.

Longstaffe, nevertheless, gave me other opportunities on his programme which was surprising because he was a very tense man, fearful about vulgarity going over the air, or what he thought might be interpreted as vulgarity. On a couple of occasions he cut my script at the last minute because he thought I was being crude.

When you were new at the job, as I was, and not too confident, it really was disconcerting to have to substitute a 'harmless gag' at the last minute. Once, I tried to go on the air with a piece which went, 'Yes, the band is going down the street and the drum major is waving his thing in his hand....'

Longstaffe went berserk. 'Disgusting! I won't have that sort of nonsense in any programme of mine.'

Unbeknown to me, while such matters were foremost in my mind, Cupid was taking aim. I was introduced to Pat, the lady destined to become my wife, by a cabaret agent who was a friend of mine. Ida Patlanski had run her own ballet-school in Johannesburg, where she was born. She was at that time in London doing a Spanish dancing act with a male partner who had suddenly walked out on her. She had been left high and dry with bookings looming, but no partner.

The agent suggested me as a substitute. Why he did this was simple. He had heard me joking about the Terry-Thomas Tango that I taught at Aida Foster's.

At first sight, Pat came over to me as a very neat, vibrant, well-read and enthusiastic little female. I decided to be truthful before she discovered the facts with her own eyes.

'Look, I don't think I'll do for you because I can't really dance flamenco,' I confessed. 'My style is capering around in Cricklewood. I don't know anything about this stuff except for the fact that I love Spanish dancing.'

'Don't worry,' she said, 'I'll show you what to do.'

Much to my amazement, she did. In the shortest time possible, I found myself clad in a white silk shirt and skin-tight trousers; and Terry hyphen Thomas had become plain Terri of the Terri and Patlanski cabaret act.

I addressed the audience in a broken Spanish accent. I

enjoyed that. While Pat was changing, after the first number, I used to say, 'Ladeez and gentlemen. The dance you just see is the tango. When a Spaniard make *loff* he is a caballero. A gentleman. But when a Mexican make *loff* he takes his partnerrrr and tearrrrs her to pieces. One minute, I show you.'

Then Pat came on and I tore her to pieces. Also myself. That act was very bad for my health. At one point, I had to take her and lift her on to my shoulder in one movement and although she was tiny, it was quite an effort. At every performance I ran a serious risk of being ruptured so, in a way, it was as well that the act was not so successful. It only lasted about three months.

But that was not the end of our partnership. As a natural course of events, Pat, nine years older than I was and twice married (the second time to a French Vicomte) moved into my flat where we continued to tear each other to pieces, Mexican-style, in private. So I was now sharing my Heath Robinson bed with a former Vicomtesse. Whizzo!

We were often skint and went from day to day taking jobs here and there. I never got depressed by this because something – a cabaret or variety booking – always turned up.

One day when we were stony broke, Pat and I had a slight tiff. It resulted in my picking her up and placing her on top of a high wardrobe. This may sound rather a tall story, but I was able to get her up there without much effort because I used the lift she had taught me in our *paso doble* routine. She managed, even in that invidious position, to turn things to her advantage. Instead of protesting and pleading to be let down, she waved two dusty tennis racquets at me.

'Look what I've found,' she yelled, 'round to the hockshop pronto, *Terri*!'

In a matter of seconds we were tearing down the road to the pawnbroker's and thence to a favourite restaurant of ours which specialized in individual steak and kidney pies. As we walked back, I said to Pat, 'What shall we do now?' And she said, 'How about a jolly game of tennis?'

(Which reminds me of the shipwrecked man on a desert island. Day after day he got thinner but resisted eating his dog. But came the fateful day when hunger got the better of him and the dog had to go.

The man was tidying up after the meal and said to himself, 'What a jolly lot of bones! Fido would have loved those.')

What prompted Pat and me to get married, one morning in 1938, I haven't the slightest idea. Perhaps we just had seven shillings and sixpence to spare – the cost of a marriage licence then – and it went to our heads.

After the brief service at Marylebone register office there was certainly no money left for a honeymoon. We just went home for a legal, Mexican-style romp.

When jobs were thin, I helped towards the housekeeping expenses by gambling. I had been a keen gambler since my Smithfield days when many salesmen owned racehorses and I'd sometimes managed to get a winner. I often played roulette and pontoon in private houses, but poker was really my game. The more hard-up I was, the better gambler I became.

Just before my marriage, I had gone alone to Nice on holiday and had enjoyed a run of good luck at the casino. One day, I was sunning myself when I suddenly leapt up with a cry. 'Christ! The casino!' I had just remembered that my season ticket to the Casino de la Jettie, which had been given to me by a friend, was running out that day.

I darted off, put on a jacket and slacks and rushed to the tables where I launched into a rather tedious game of roulette. I had worked out a simple method. I just backed two columns for an even sum of money so that if I won on a column I would win two and lose one.

On this particular day, luck was against me. In no time at all, I was down to my last hundred francs. If I lost this, the outlook was grim. I would have to curtail my holiday and go home. I put all my money on number eleven – my favourite number – knowing that I would lose. For a minute I had one of those blanks of the mind: I couldn't remember the French for eleven.

The answer came from the croupier as I got up to leave: '*Onze, rouge, impair et manque.*' I'd won! Enough to stay in the South of France until the end of summer. Lovely!

Back in London, Pat and I got a steady job with Don Rico. He was a friend of hers who ran a women's orchestra. Dancer Pat was taken on as a pianist and I gradually eased myself into the show as compère. Apart from Don Rico himself, and some Russian fellow in charge of the music, I was the only man.

We all used to meet at a central point in London. From there we'd be transported by coach to a summer coastal resort. A feature of the evening was a talent contest that I organized, sometimes for singing, other times for acting.

The acting one was a huge joke. I used to introduce this Russian chappie as an important talent scout from Elstree. Then I would persuade people from the audience to come up and read a letter which stated that they had been left one million pounds. They had to react to this news, giving their own interpretations of shock and surprise. The reactions were usually so gauche that it all turned out too much for the old Russian. He would nearly choke to death with laughter, and this set me off as well. We just fell over each other. Then the audience would catch it too.

The singing competition was more serious. I remember, at Southend-on-Sea, that a girl with a really fine voice presented herself. She was a local waitress named Winifred Scott and it was just like those traditional Hollywood musicals of the time because we decided to employ her immediately. The next night there she was, the star of the show. The extraordinary thing was that, despite her magnificent voice, with its great style and attack, which had sent shivers down my spine the first time I heard it, she did not go on to become famous.

Her husband, Jeffrey, a tram-driver, was probably the reason. He insisted on being with her at every rehearsal when decisions were being discussed and making himself objectionable.

I blush when I think of some of the things I did in cabaret for thirty bob a week. It was masochistic. I was footsore from pounding the pavements of the West End calling on theatrical agents who, if I was lucky, would book me into ghastly clubs like the Paradise, known picturesquely in the business as 'upholstered sewers'.

As often as not the slings and arrows of outrageous fortune would be hurled at one's head in the form of rolled-up table napkins, accompanied by boos, whistles, cat-calls and table thumping.

When you are starting, that kind of thing can rock you badly. I had to give a toothy grin, pretend it wasn't happening and go on with my act. After a few such dates, I learned how to project myself against a background of constant chatter. Only in retrospect does that sort of thing become a marvellous experience.

Life as a married couple, was not as pleasant as it had been when Pat and I were living in sin. I was not at all happy about Pat, actually, because apart from everything else, she began to have affairs with other men from very early on in the marriage. Naturally this did not please me one bit and there were angry scenes. That's when I discovered that she had a terrible temper. There had been no screaming matches before we were married, but afterwards she flew into the most shocking rages. It needed some believing to hear her in action.

'Come up and get your lunch at once, or I'll throw it in the dustbin,' she would scream from the mews window at my retreating back, as I strolled towards our local boozer, the Queen's Arms.

How such a lot of noise could be made by such a tiny person was incredible. To this day I'm not sure what most of it was all about. Years later, after we'd been divorced but were on amicable terms again, Pat put it down to ill-health — hers!

I began to play life as it came. In 1939 I was beginning to get somewhere both in cabaret and in variety, so lots of opportunities for extra-marital fun presented themselves, which needless to say, I took. As my wife was blatantly having affairs, I felt rather inclined to do the same. Talk about tit for tat.

(Which brings to mind the time I was in a bar and the barmaid said, 'Aren't you Terry-Thomas?' I said, 'Yes. Not to be confused with any other Thomas you might have heard of.' 'I thought I recognized you,' she said. 'You're the chap who knows a lot of stories.' 'Yes, I know quite a few.' 'So do I,' she said, 'and I bet I can give you tit for tat.' So I said, 'TAT!')

When ENSA was formed, a lot of artistes who had been out of work immediately presented themselves for a job. Pat and I were among them and in the shortest space of time I had fixed for both of us to go to France with a show. To be truthful I had wangled myself in charge of that cabaret because I had a special girl-friend in the company called Marilyn, daughter of the famous dancer, Marilyn Miller. She had long legs, deep bosoms, a beautiful classic face and a stunning complexion. She sang reasonably well, too. I was just knocked off my feet by her.

Obviously it was not at all easy having your wife and your girl-friend in the same show. I decided I had to get rid of one of them. And that was Pat. I arranged for ENSA to switch her to another company, back in Britain. I don't think she had any idea of my affair with Marilyn.

After Pat left, the show did not go on quite as often as it should have, because Marilyn and I were 'rehearsing new numbers' upstairs in my room.

Until then there had only been talk and speculation in Britain about the possibilities of a war with Germany. Behind the lines it was different. You could see that the French knew war was inevitable. There was bizarre evidence in the red-light district....

One night an RAF pal took Marilyn and me to a well-known brothel in Rheims where the atmosphere was said to be highly sophisticated. It was very dark in there, the only spots of light being directed high up at a series of beautifully painted murals hung around the perimeter of the room. At first glance the delicate pastel colours seemed to depict old-fashioned sylvan scenes. But when you studied the paintings in detail, you realized they actually showed German soldiers, sailors and airmen – some well-known faces among them – all stuck into each other, round the room, in a daisy chain.

Madame pointed at them. 'Dirty Boche!' she spat, her eyes blazing with contempt.

She then took us into a sitting room where two naked young girls sang a corny RAF song in broken English while performing together for our benefit.

I thought it a rather jolly affair, but Marilyn burst into tears. She felt the girls were too young to be in that place doing that to each other.

We started to leave, pushing our way through groups of giggling French tarts who were moving from room to room with towels draped around them. At this point, Madame took me to one side and said, 'I hope *you're* going to stay.'

The idea did not suit me at all. I knew I was on a pretty good thing with Marilyn and I didn't like to think she had been left with the handsome RAF officer. So I said, 'Pardon Madame! I'm the chief of the show and it wouldn't be a good thing for me to be found in here.'

We scarpered, said ta-ta to the RAF officer and went back to our hotel. Discreetly, I went up to my room first and opened a bottle of the delicious champagne that was produced in the Rheims district.

I waited for Marilyn to join me. I waited. And I waited.

She returned at last, hours later. She had been held in conversation by a silly old conjuror who had sensed we were up to no good and had done everything he possibly could to prevent her joining me. Little did he know the endurance of the chap with the gift of the gap. Eventually time told the old man he had to have his sleep. But I didn't!

The next evening I sat in front of a café with Marilyn

watching the aeroplanes dog-fight over Rheims. I wasn't frightened by the crazily lighted sky or by the noise because it all seemed so unreal. It couldn't go on. Soon it must stop.

It soon did. That was the Phoney War. Not long after that, Hitler marched through and round the Maginot Line and in no time was doing his mad gig opposite the white cliffs of Dover.

When Marilyn and I got back to London to go our separate ways, although sad at the parting, it was with great gusto that I threw myself into my work for ENSA.

From now on it was obvious we were all going to be kept rather busy.

2 *Technical Hitch*

'Look, Sir Seymour, there's no point in farting at thunder.' I made this explosive observation one day after Sir Seymour Hicks and I had had yet another of our differences. The elderly, much revered actor gave me a pained look. With Dame Lillian Braithwaite, another stanchion of the theatre, Sir Seymour was responsible for the running of the Drama Section of ENSA at the Theatre Royal, Drury Lane, where I had been put in charge of the Cabaret Section.

Right from the beginning, Sir Seymour and I seemed to find ourselves always arguing over trivial matters. He constantly criticized me, but I knew I was right. The proof of the pudding, in my opinion, was our outstanding success with the troops.

I was turning out good shows, sophisticated, impeccable and highly polished. Some very charming dancers called the Gainsborough Girls made up our chorus line. Every one of them was classy, or if they weren't they certainly made sure that they looked and sounded that way. Not like the tough-nut chorus girls you normally came across.

During the show violinist Eugene Pini played light classics beautifully and I told some rather smooth stories. It was a smart turnout altogether and the troops loved it.

Much to my amazement, because I considered I was doing such important work for ENSA, I received a cunningly worded invitation to join the Army. It would have seemed rather rude and ungrateful to refuse, so I accepted with dignity, if not enthusiasm.

I tore myself away from my weeping and clinging ENSA party and joined the Royal Corps of Signals, at Osset, in Yorkshire. I had scarcely been there twenty-four hours when a sergeant asked me my number. 'Mayfair 0736,' I said, facetiously. He gave me a slip of paper upon which was written 2389211. 'You ain't Terry-Thomas any more,' he said. 'You are now just an effing number.' I leaned forward over his table and said, 'Yes mate. Number one!'

Then followed an awful five weeks. I found myself marching over a mile to breakfast at the time I normally would have been going to bed. What a dead loss anyway, because I never ate breakfast. Osset was very near the Arctic Circle, or at least it felt like it.

The Army brought out in me my two strongest characteristics: I hated to be under-estimated and I was extremely competitive. There were many things I loathed, yet I was also frightfully keen. At the end of my preliminary training, I was given the Senior Soldier Flash 'A' for being the best recruit. I was made a corporal.

Although I had thrown myself into the strict training and willingly done all that was asked of me, it took a toll of my health. A nervous stomach turned me into a non-stop eater and a duodenal ulcer was prodded into activity. I was also having trouble with my ears. 'You don't stand a hope in hell of getting a commission,' gloated an Army doctor.

So I was down-graded and although, by now, I had become a very keen soldier, I didn't really mind because I had met impresario George Black (of George and Alfred Black).

He was then a captain and had just started an Army entertainment called *Stars in Battledress* with people like Charlie Chester, Peter Cavanagh, Arthur Haynes, Peter Ustinov, Kenny Morris, Sid Millward and Michael Denison. My 'star' was rising, for George invited me to join this illustrious team and started an association that was to go on long after the war was over. When my obituary is eventually printed in the papers, mark my words, it will say that George Black discovered me.

But it had been back in 1940, with ENSA in Norwich, that something happened which was to change my life and make my fortune. Norwich was a ghastly place. Probably still is. I had been to see Richard Tauber in *Old Chelsea* and when I came out of the theatre, it was snowing heavily. I trudged across the street to the pub opposite for a noggin.

In the warm, smoky haze of the public bar, I happened to hear a BBC announcer who became famous for what happened that night. There was an air raid whilst he was reading the news and a bomb hit Broadcasting House. True to the tradition of the BBC, he calmly continued the programme as if nothing had happened.

Thinking about this situation gave me the idea for *Technical Hitch* – the television sketch that was to be my most successful act and make me a household name. As *Technical Hitch* played such an enormous part in my career, I had better describe it in detail.

Dressed in a faultless dinner jacket, with clove carnation in place, I introduced the piece as my impression as to how far a BBC announcer would go to cover up a technical hitch. For in the true blue tradition of the BBC, the show has to go on come what may (or June or July for that matter).

The sketch opened with me as the announcer rushing into the studio from the wings shouting loudly for someone to 'pay off the taxi' as I searched frantically for the script and records which were needed for the programme that was about to go on the air. With ballet-like leaps I bounded round the stage coming to a dead halt when the red light went on. I whispered loudly to the pianist to start the introductory music and – with a sickly smile – calmly informed the listeners that I was their old friend, Freddie Featherstonehaugh-Bumleigh (by the way, Featherstonehaugh was pronounced Feston-Hay) with another selection of simply spiffing gramophone records.

'The first one I'm going to play is Al Jolson singing "Sonny Boy",' I said, and then broke into song doing an appalling impersonation of Jolson.

When I got to the end, almost collapsing, I mouthed hysterically to the pianist. 'Where are the records?' The pianist – over the top himself, by now – mouthed back that I should go and get stuffed, or some such telling phrase.

Three or four equally dreadful impersonations followed, of Paul Robeson, Yma Sumac and Richard Tauber, and all the time I did a lot of rushing about the stage searching for some solution. At last, inspiration came and I signalled the pianist to play an arpeggio whilst I simulated the breaking down of the turn-table by making squeaking noises and clicking my thumb against my front teeth.

I stopped the pianist and said, 'I'm sorry. We seem to have got a slight technical hitch.'

I signed off by singing a fairly straight song using the voice of Hutch.

The sketch was first performed four years after I had conceived the idea, at an Army show base at Olympia. Although it ran for twenty-six minutes – far too long – *Technical Hitch*, with its racy style, was a winner. The audience lapped it up and I was 'made' overnight.

After the Olympia début, I went out in a *Stars in Battledress* show with Eugene Pini, John Duncan (a well-known tenor) and a string sextet. As we went around the country, I polished the act until I had a version which lasted exactly twelve-and-a-half minutes.

By the end of the war, I was a sergeant on the staff of the *Stars in Battledress* depot in Upper Grosvenor Street. I had been overworking and was not feeling at all well. I wanted to get out of the Army as quickly as possible and went to see various people to see if they could help. Nobody could until an entertainments officer said to me, 'Why on earth do you want to get out? I can tell you a way to stay in and be out at the same time.

'Go up to your colonel and ask him for twenty-eight days' compasssionate leave. At the end of it, you report back and he gives you another twenty-eight. You can get in some variety dates and you'll be getting Army pay as well.'

'Goodness gracious me! Well, thank you very much. Cheers!' I said and off I rushed to see first my colonel and then George Black who was now back in civilian life and once more connected to the Moss Empire circuit.

Very soon I was touring the country in all the best variety theatres, after opening at the Palace, Blackpool. It was a perfect arrangement. My pianist, Harry Sutcliffe, had been demobbed with the rank of colonel. Now here he was, Col Sutcliffe, accompanying a 'perpetually-on-leave' sergeant round the halls. It was quite incredible what I got away with in those last days of my Army service. What a wheeze! Once a month I had to report back to camp, wangle more leave and then catch a train to rejoin the show.

When I was demobbed in April, 1946, who would have foreseen that within six months I would be performing before the King and Queen on the stage of the London Palladium? Certainly not I!

It was in October of that same year that George Black put me into the Prince of Wales Theatre, at £45 a week, in Sid Field's *Piccadilly Hayride*. To my surprise, I was made compère of the show. It gave me a valuable position; really, it gave me the whole show. Sid – a very funny man – never came into close contact with the audience but as host of the show I did, right from the beginning. I was able to introduce *Technical Hitch* into my final spot after presenting Robert Lamouret (a ventriloquist with a talking duck called Dudule), dancers Alan and Blanche Lund and the Ross Sisters.

Sid Field was easy to get on with; a marvellous person to have around, very friendly and warm. Even though he was the star of the show, he seemed not to mind that the newspapers gave such a lot of coverage to me. I even had a two-page article in *Punch*.

'Comic is Picked for Variety' was the headline in the *Daily Express* when the cast was announced for the Royal Variety Performance in November. 'Terry-Thomas, who came back to civilian life from the Army where he made a big name for himself in service shows, will appear in an all-star Royal Variety Show.' Then followed the list: Nat Jackley, Nat Mills and Bobbie, Arthur Askey, Sid Field, Harry Lester and his Hayseeds, Jewel and Warriss ...

I was an overnight star. My wages went up to a couple of hundred pounds a week and I was in great demand. Between breaks I used to go out on a lorry, with a piano and pianist, Derek Scott, on board, to do other bookings in the West End. I took on so much extra work that the tight schedule made it necessary to employ a secretary, Joan Haigh. If there was any doubt whether one of these extra performances could be fitted in, Joan would have to do a dummy run in the lorry from the theatre to wherever I was going. If it was to be the Dorchester, for instance, she would rush through the hotel, stop-watch in hand, to the room where they wanted me to appear, to see if there would be time.

With more and more of these additional bookings, lots of BBC work, plus the prestige of standing in at the Palladium for a few nights when Tommy Trinder was indisposed, I considered it a poor week if I earned less than 500 quid.

I found myself in a shocking state by the time *Piccadilly Hayride* closed. It had run for eighteen months and turned me into a star. The wages of stardom, however, were a resurrected stomach ulcer and a bad case of nervous exhaustion.

I went to see my doctor in Queensgate who whisked me off to see a man named Mutch in Harley Street. His name set me wondering how much he would charge me and how much more ill-health I could take. After examining me, Mutch said, 'There's not much I can do for you. You just need a rest. I suggest you go to Tring where you will live on only orange juice for three weeks.'

'Only orange juice? That's not much,' I wailed.

Mutch grinned: 'You'll enjoy it thoroughly.'

Before I knew what was happening, I was installed in the famous health farm existing on three oranges a day. It was terrible. Unbearable. Salvation came in the form of two fellow guests, Sir Bernard and Lady Docker. While taking our recommended afternoon walks in the fresh air we used to slip away in the famous gold-plated Daimler for the odd clandestine scone. I often wondered if the Dockers, always larger than life, managed to shrink a bit while they were there. They certainly helped my three weeks to pass painlessly. At the end, after all the rigid fasting, I felt well enough to go back to London to take over from Ted Ray at the Palladium, during which show I had to introduce the Brazilian Bombshell, Hollywood film-star Carmen Miranda.

Carmen sang her songs well, but she wasn't much of a talker, nor a comedienne, so I didn't enjoy performing with her. She was supposed to be glamorous, but for me, the glamour stopped immediately below her exotic, fruit-decorated head-dresses. As a matter of fact, I thought she was hideous. Only recently I read in a high-class glossy that she used not to wear anything underneath as she wanted no restrictions to her movements while she was dancing. Now they tell me!

Talking about panties being removed, I'm told that today's liberated women actually slip their underwear off and throw it at Tom Jones and Julio Iglesias to show appreciation for a song.

Things have obviously moved on since my day. The first time I witnessed mass fan worship was when Johnnie Ray and I appeared on the same bill at the Palladium. When he 'cried' during his performance, the women in the audience were content to drown his singing by merely screaming and sighing in ecstasy.

In 1947 I had made my first television appearance from Alexandra Palace in *Stars in Your Eyes*. From then on I was often given five or six-minute spots that were slotted in as fill-gaps between programmes.

To Town with Terry was the name of my own BBC radio programme which was broadcast regularly during 1948 and 1949. My second radio series was *Top of the Town* which followed the formula of the first and ran for two years. But I was never totally satisfied with either production. The perfectionist in me always made me aware of anything that was less than first class.

Far more exciting was my half-hour television show, *How Do You View?* It was the first-ever comedy series on British television. The year: 1951.

The BBC had tried to insist that we played *How Do You View?* to a live audience, but very firmly I said no. I did not want the home viewers' enjoyment spoilt by controlled laughter in the studio. I knew I was well able to time my delivery to allow for the people sitting at home to have their chortle without missing the next joke. While most comedians found it impossible to be funny without an audience to play to, I was adamant that we had no need of one. And I was right, of course.

I concocted the idea and was lucky enough to get two splendid writers, Sid Colin and Tolly Rothwell. The programme opened on me in close-up with a very broad smile saying the now classic lines: 'How do you view? Are you frightfully well? You ARE? Oh, good show!'

As I said this, I looked directly into the camera. This greeting was extremely difficult, but once I had mastered it the rest of the show was a piece of cake. I used to rehearse it in front of the studio mirrors. After this introduction, I continued in a very light-hearted way to present the rest of the cast.

In this show I was supposed to be a man-about-town complete with butler, a very decrepit character named Moulton. He was played by the late Herbert C Walton who was such a dedicated performer that he never got out of character once he was in the studio. In the canteen or in the lift he called me Terry, but once in the studio he never addressed me other than by saying 'Master Terry', as in the script.

Avril Angers was Rosie Lee, 'the girl with the tea', Janet

Brown was Miss Hap, my secretary. And Janet's husband, the late Peter Butterworth, played my chauffeur, Lockit. The running joke was that, although I had a chauffeur, I hadn't a car. Peter acted his part so well and so sympathetically that every week we involved our listeners to the extent that they sent us loads of spare parts. Eventually, there were so many we could have actually built ourselves a jalopy.

Later in the show there was another spot where Leslie Mitchell (of Movietone News fame) used to interview me playing some strange characters such as the Rank Organization's gong-man, a broken-down boxer or a Beefeater. (The Queen saw Leslie and me do the Beefeater one on her first-ever visit to a TV studio.) The show's musical spot was filled by guests such as Dickie Valentine, Adelaide Hall, Lita Roza and, once or twice, by Jimmy Young. Jimmy played the piano and was a pop-singer of hits like 'Unchained Melody' and 'Too Young', and I liked his work very much.

We spent three days rehearsing, then went out live. In spite of the fact that props sometimes fell down, doors didn't open, or I would ad-lib and distract my colleagues, we had found the most marvellous formula which couldn't go wrong. I was paid £100 for each fortnightly show.

Apart from the opening catch-phrase, suddenly everybody was talking about the gap between my teeth, my monocle, the fancy waistcoats I wore and the seven-inch cigarette holders I used.

The gap in my smile I was born with. That could hardly be called a contrived gimmick, but the other three things certainly were. The monocle had entered my life quite early on for another of my schoolboy idols had been Erich von Stroheim. The Austrian actor did things to me. I was so mad keen on him that I spent a lot of my time doing my Stroheim impersonation. A monocle, of course, was part of him. I used the glass face from a watch to stick in my eye. Years later I used a real monocle when I impersonated Richard Tauber in

Technical Hitch. Gradually I began to use it more and more off-stage, too. Not just for pretension. I needed it, to read the wine lists in poorly lit restaurants!

I first started wearing fancy waistcoats as a young man. People had always remarked most favourably on them so it seemed a good idea to adopt the distinctive style for my appearance on television.

My TV waistcoats were made for me by a firm called Wings, in Piccadilly, at my own expense. The average waistcoat then cost £25. I suppose a similar thing today would be at least £150. I used to bet two to one that you could not stand for three minutes outside the display window of Wings without hearing my name mentioned.

I had waistcoats made of silk, satin, suede, bearskin, velvet, wool ... and there was even one made of white mink. When I made a personal appearance at the Odeon, Dalston, in connection with my film *Make Mine Mink*, a local furrier who had secretly acquired my measurements from my tailor presented me with the waistcoat: one hundred poundsworth of American white EMBA mink. It was extremely comfortable and certainly in-fur-iated a few women friends of mine who positively coveted it.

I had a wonderful surprise one day when a parcel arrived containing a grey waistcoat with diamond buttons. Caruso's widow had sent it to me, saying it was made in 1850. I never wore it because it wasn't big enough, but I still treasure it.

My favourite waistcoat of all – black velvet with flowers embroidered in silk, cost a mighty £40, and another splendid affair, made of black moiré with gold fern embroidery, that I performed in at a Christmas party for the Royal Household at Windsor Castle, took the eye of King George VI. He was most amused by it when we chatted afterwards, especially when I said I called it the Mudlark. 'Have you seen my show on television?' I asked him. 'Don't be bloody silly,' the King said. 'Of course I have.'

I still have about seventy of the most beautiful of the waistcoats. And I still get the occasional request to donate one for a charity function.

The long cigarette holder became part of my stock in trade in the late Forties after I had discovered the most irresistible holder in Dunhill's. It was slightly outré because it was made of lacquered, black whangee (a type of bamboo) with a gold band twisting neatly round it. To keep the smoke out of my eyes at the card table and also to prevent nicotine-stained fingers, which I hated, I had used a holder for smoking for years, but never such a long one. To get accustomed to using the seven-inch one before I appeared with it on television, I would go for walks near my home while smoking with it, just to get my eye in. It wanted a bit of nerve to use a holder of that shape and size in real life.

Funnily enough, I had given up smoking in 1945, on doctor's orders. I'd been a dozen-a-day man up to then. So when I was seen on TV or in my cabaret act with a lighted du Maurier in a holder, for me it was only another stage prop, I wasn't really 'smoking'. I used to time my act by the holder. Holding it in my hand and taking the occasional puff, it lasted ten minutes.

Once *How Do You View?* had caught on, fans started sending me gifts of holders. One was in the shape of a TV aerial with holes for five fags at a time. When I played a friendly villain in the film *Tom Thumb* (1958) – my second favourite of all the movies that I appeared in – I used a holder with holes for two cigarettes at once. It doubled as a catapult.

I still have about forty holders. Naturally, there were a few casualties among my collection. And some 'went missing'.

It was the theft in 1960 of the famous and most valuable holder in my collection that got the headlines. Three years earlier, it had been on show at the International Watch and Jewellery Trade Fair, at Albert Hall, where the total exhibits were valued at five million pounds.

'Made for Terry-Thomas,' read the brochure, 'this £2,000 cigarette holder is of black-lacquered whangee wood with 18-carat yellow gold spiral band, a star of diamonds set throughout its length and millegrain set ferrels at each end.'

Labour MP Bessie Braddock was a good friend of mine. She was warm and lively, a quite marvellous person who lit up a room when she walked in. She had invited me to lunch at the House of Commons, and got me involved in various charity 'do's' in her constituency, Liverpool. It was at one of these 'do's' that my holder was pinched.

I had gone to Liverpool to compère a midnight variety show at the Odeon Cinema, London Road. During the evening, I was constantly pestered by a young man who wanted to appear in the programme. I kept pointing out to him that we had too many artistes already; that it would be madness to put anybody else on.

Later that night, when I returned to my dressing-room, I discovered that my cigarette holder which I had left there – the one with the forty-two diamonds and the gold spiral band – had gone.

'Two men held' was the headline in the Press, a fortnight later. The police had found gold parts of the holder, and forty diamonds, hidden in a roll of carpet at the home of the young chap who had tried so hard to get himself included on the bill.

He was completely and utterly unknown then. Today, he is one of Britain's most popular comedians, frequently seen on television.

It was a silly jape on his part to take my holder as a souvenir because it cost me an enormous amount of time and travel attending court, quite apart from my solicitor's fees.

He has never mentioned the incident to me, but I still have the newspaper cuttings of the case in which he pleaded guilty at Liverpool Crown Court to stealing my diamond-studded holder and was placed on probation for two years. His defence said he had taken it in a moment of pique, rather than with dishonest intent. He had expected to take part in the charity show, but had not been called upon. An unemployed sales-man was found guilty of feloniously receiving two of the diamonds from the holder.

*

The London Palladium was without doubt the British Mecca of variety. I felt more at home there than on any other stage because I was able to use broader and more sophisticated material than normal. Every artiste was terrified of 'dying the death' at the Palladium. It was such a prestige booking that if your performance was less than one hundred per cent, it could badly damage your career. Yet I had no more 'butter-flies' when I played there than I had at the Golders Green Hippodrome. Indeed, I found the Palladium more relaxing despite the fact that Val Parnell, the Palladium boss, was very nasty to me in the beginning. The older I got, and the more successful, the nicer he became.

Val (who was Noele Gordon's boyfriend for many years) had a reputation for being the toughest man in the business. He was! He once disagreed with Jerry Desmonde, Sid Field's straight-man, over some trifling matter. After Sid's death, Val never used Jerry again. As Jerry was as big a name as Sid Field had been, this took a bit of believing, but that's how Val was.

The only occasion I was not happy at the Palladium was when I topped the bill in *Fun and the Fair* – at £1,400 a week – with George Formby and Billy Cotton's Band. The morning after we opened in October 1953, the producer, Charles Henry, called me to a rehearsal and said, 'Why do you think you flopped?'

I said, 'I don't think I did flop. But I certainly didn't do as well as I'd like to have done.'

I knew it was the running order that had blunted my efforts. On the posters, in equal type, George Formby's name was on the left, Billy Cotton's in the centre, and mine on the right. This meant that Formby played the penultimate spot. I closed the show with my impression of a sergeant-major imperso-nating Noël Coward.

The trouble was, George Formby put the audience in a certain mood which made them non-receptive to whoever followed. This was his comeback after a long illness. The year before, he had had to quit his West End show *Zip Goes a Million*, because of heart trouble.

'George Formby back in good health and spirits ... we were one big happy family rejoicing at the return of the prodigal,' wrote the *Sunday Express* theatre critic, putting the situation neatly into one sentence.

Even though the closing act was the star spot, I felt on this occasion that my being there was an anti-climax. I told Charles Henry: 'George Formby is really the star of this show. He should go on last. Put him where he belongs, and give me a chance.'

But Charles liked my work and he wasn't keen on Formby's. 'What?' he said. 'Put him last with all those bloody awful parrot stories?'

So the order was not changed. I continued to end the show and I had to work very hard indeed to raise the audience up again, and keep them up, after much-loved Formby had appeared. I never performed on the same bill with George Formby again.

Nevertheless, George and I got on well during the run. Although I did not, personally, find him a *funny* man, he was a very good sort. When we had opened in Blackpool, I had organized horse races along the sands and George, a former jockey, had beaten me every time. By now I owned a dozen horses which were kept stabled at St Anne's and my horse-shows raised a lot of money for charity.

I remember one race when Jimmy Edwardes, Bonar Colleano and Susan Shaw (all appearing in other Blackpool shows) were on the line-up with George and me.

Jimmy won. The race was a mile long and finished outside the Queen's Hotel, where I was staying. I had led the way and was convinced that I had the race in my pocket, but no, it was not to be. Jim gradually caught up on me and beat me by about twenty yards.

I presented him with the trophy, a silver cup commemorating the day of The Bastille Stakes. It was my birthday, and 14 July, as you probably know, was the day when the Bastille in Paris was stormed by the mob and all the incarcerated unfortunates regained their liberty; we had some very good

French champagne to celebrate the event.

My favourite time at the Palladium was in the 1958 show *Large as Life* when I appeared as one of the Three Musketeers with Harry Secombe, Eric Sykes and Hattie Jacques. We looked forward to every performance and not once did we get through the sketch without being overcome with mirth. There was one very clever moment behind a screen, just an ordinary simple screen that you might find in an old-fashioned drawing room or studio.

As we fenced, we moved across the stage until we were hidden by this screen. The audience could not see us at all, but they could see the swords waving in the air. We then moved out on the other side, but now we weren't holding any swords; they were still waving about behind the screen. When we noticed we no longer held the swords, we rushed back behind the screen to get them and continued the sketch.

Harry Secombe, I mean *Sir* Harry, was a great character who knew when to be serious. Not like some comedians who felt compelled to act the giddy goat the whole time. But hark who's talking! As the long Palladium season went on, I spent more and more time in Harry's dressing-room telling jokes. Sometimes (as Harry remembers it) we were there until three in the morning.

He was a marvellous audience and much appreciated my cockney stories, most of which I'd picked up as a boy. I used to laugh at them as much as he did.

Harry must have told fellow-goon, Peter Sellers, about our sessions because when I phoned Peter in Hollywood, he said, 'Ah, T-T, the *raconteur*.'

The year after my first pantomime, *Humpty Dumpty* at the Palladium (with Noele Gordon as Principal Boy and Norman Evans as Dame), I was offered another pantomime part – the Honourable Idle Jack, in *Dick Whittington*. That one was in South Africa. I took it because the idea of sunshine for Christmas appealed to me. And it would give my wife Pat the chance to visit her relations.

But after the Palladium and its sleek production, playing in

Dick Whittington in Johannesburg, really was going from the sublime to the ridiculous. Amateurism was not in it. The whole thing was so tatty and unrehearsed it was pathetic.

It was whispered that somebody had acquired the scenery cheap, and one could well believe it. The sets did not fit the stage and it took ages to build each scene. Members of the cast had to keep popping out in front of the curtain ad-libbing like mad while hysterical stage hands struggled to secure the errant back-cloths. At twenty minutes past midnight, a woman in the audience was heard to say, 'I think today's show is better than yesterday's.' Somebody must have found it entertaining!

Johannesburg as a place did not grab me at all. I found it even more depressing than Norwich or Finchley. New York, on the other hand, which Pat and I had just visited, had been much better value. They had booked me for my archetypal Englishman image and I intended to be the kind of cove they thought we were all like. I set sail from Liverpool with Pat – and sixty waistcoats.

The papers made much of the fact that I would earn the equivalent of £357 for my first TV show in America. They had discovered that the BBC had paid me only £100 a programme for my first *How Do You View?* series, and that I had demanded £150 a time for the second series.

For my TV début, on the Ed Sullivan show, I wore a gold-embroidered waistcoat. 'I can't tell you,' I told that vast audience of transatlantic viewers, 'how wonderful it is to be in this great city of ... of ...' (I fumbled in my pocket for a slip of paper) 'New York!'

(This line is the perfect example of a piece of material that, if played right, can stop the show.)

Ed Sullivan did not seem particularly bright to me; he seemed to make a mess of introducing his guests. On the previous Sunday I had switched on the television to see what his show was like. And this is how I heard myself announced as a forthcoming attraction.

'Don't forget to watch next week, folks. We've got a

wonderful show for you. We have England's top television star, Tommy Tucker.'

When I did my season at the Waldorf Astoria's Wedgwood Room, I found that live US audiences were much slower than I was used to. They took an awful long time to see the subtle stuff. But didn't they enjoy it when they did! They gave themselves an extra pat on the back for spotting it. Here's one that was often received in silence – then to be followed by laughter.

A lay preacher, who was a great favourite with everybody, used to preach regularly in a certain hall. But after some years he was suddenly booted out for some trifling thing. It couldn't have been for anything very much – he was over 70.

When the time came for him to say goodbye, he said: 'Brethren, as I pass through you when I leave this hall for the last time, I should like you to know that I have a little sprig of mistletoe underneath my shirt-tails.'

The *Evening Standard* had given me a cable card in order that I could send home my snap impressions of New York. They printed these in a series called 'The Velvet Collared Englishmen in the Asphalt Jungle.' In one report, I wrote: 'My American agent was surprised I was a funny-man. It seems he thought I was a ventriloquist. My wife, who is on the small side, is very angry. She feels she was mistaken for the dummy.'

Dear old Pat. We were always at each other's throats, and being mutually unfaithful, but we shared a lot of good times. In New York she insisted on wearing a hat that was frightening. It really made her look awful but she thought it was just right for the wife of the current toast-of-the-town from Britain. The colour of it was the worst thing – throbbing pink! But she wouldn't take any notice of what I said and continued to wear it everywhere.

One morning, however, when she waved down a taxi by Central Park, the cabbie said, 'Hey lady, where DID you get that hat?' She asked, 'Why?' And he said, 'Well, excuse me for saying so, but it don't do nothin' for yuh.' The hat was never seen again.

Back in Britain 'The Adventures of Terry-Thomas' started appearing weekly in picture-strip form in *Film Fun*. I was elected TV's second most outstanding personality of the year (Richard Dimbleby being the first), and I began popping up as a guest on all sorts of TV programmes.

I also had my own 'specials'. Leslie Hutchinson, 'Hutch', who was a great mate of mine, appeared on one TV 'special'. He had just started his introduction to a song when he suddenly leant sideways and said directly into camera, 'Hello, Boo Boo, this one is for you.'

I was mystified because that was not in the script. When I asked him about it afterwards, his face creased into a big smile and he told me he knew that his friend, Edwina, Countess Mountbatten, would be looking in so he had decided, at the last minute, to dedicate the song to her.

Hutch was the greatest of charmers. He exuded fun and well-being and (especially) sex appeal. Once, at the Finsbury Park Empire, I heard someone say admiringly, as we stood in the wings watching Hutch's performance, 'He's playing that piano just as though it were a woman.'

The stage manager said, 'Well, it's a female piano.' The piano had Queen Anne legs.

On the evening of the Sunday that war broke out, Pat and I went to stay in a lovely house in north London where we were entertained lavishly. Hutch was there too, and we had a marvellous evening with Hutch and Pat vying with each other on the piano.

When it came time for bed, we went upstairs and Hutch said, 'I'm in here' and entered a very beautifully furnished bedroom. It was the most feminine bedroom I had ever seen.

He opened a suitcase and took out a large bottle of Chanel No 5. With great panache, he whipped the clothes off the bed (which put me in mind of a conjuror removing the tablecloth from a fully laid table without moving any of the cutlery, china or crystal) and then, very deliberately, he showered the sheets from the bottle of perfume. There wasn't any doubt what was going to be happening for the next hour or so.

With a wicked grin, Hutch said goodnight to us and, gently humming 'Begin the Beguine', he disappeared down the stairs.

Both Hutch and I would have been very surprised if we had been told that, within just a few years, I would be arranging parts in films for him, the first one being *The Brass Monkey*. I shot up very quickly after my success at the Prince of Wales and soon worked myself into a position of influence in films about show business.

I also appeared in *The Brass Monkey* and decided that Carole Landis, who starred with Herbert Lom and Carroll Levis, was one of the most intelligent women I had ever come across.

Thornton Freeland, the director, said to her one day, 'Let's get this thing in the can. Can we work faster?'

American-born Carole replied, 'Not unless you can print on the film, "Sorry folks about the poor quality, but we had to do it in a hurry."'

One year later, when she was only twenty-nine, Carole's life came to a tragic end. Following an unhappy friendship with Rex Harrison, she committed suicide.

'Doing the halls' as I did for many years, one quickly got to know which places were pushovers and which ones were tricky because the British sense of humour varied from town to town. Bradford audiences, for instance, were keen to receive subtle humour and got most enthusiastic when they did.

Dorothy Squires once shared the top of the bill with me at Bradford and on the first night she invited me to her dressing-room and sent out for a bottle of champagne, to toast our week's success. We did have a good week, too, but I knew we would. Bradford, as far as I was concerned, was one of the best bookings of the lot.

On the other hand, in Nottingham, which after all was only a few miles away, they were not nearly so easy to please. Parts of the south, like Eastbourne and Bournemouth, were good. But there were certain theatres I grew to dread, the Hackney Empire being one. Very difficult audience in Hackney, most unfriendly lot. Yet the Glasgow Empire, the booking proverbially approached with trepidation by a large number of my colleagues, had the reverse effect on me. I loved appearing there.

The worst place for me was Norwich. I'd hated it in wartime and it was just as dreary after the war. A friend of mine, a London jeweller, came to watch my show there and made this astute observation: 'If I were in Show Business,' he told me at the end of the show, 'I would use Norwich to test out material. Anything they laughed at, I'd cut!'

For a special reason I remember the Dudley Hippodrome. There was a Salvation Army woman who worked as a waitress in the hotel in front of the theatre. She was always muddling her words, with hilarious results. One morning she said, 'I've joost seen the Earl of Doodley. He was wearing his binolackers round his neck.'

Another time she rushed into the kitchen and said, 'Disgoostin'! That Mr and Mrs Brown ought to know better. I've joost taken their breakfast oop to their room. And what do you think was on the roog by the bed? A great big preservative.'

Once when I went to a trade exhibition to make a personal appearance, the north country organizer greeted me apologetically.

'I'm afraid you'll find it pretty rough going,' he said. 'We've had comics here before but the audience hardly took a blind bit of notice of them.'

I couldn't understand what he was talking about because I didn't have any difficulty in making them roar with laughter. When I came off, what do you think the chap said to me? 'Ah, you were lucky. That's the best audience we've ever had.'

I don't think I ever 'died the death' but there were a lot of occasions when hecklers tried hard to ruin my act. One night at the Savoy, when Princess Margaret was watching the show, there was some trouble with barracking. I said to her afterwards, 'I'm sorry about the unpleasantness, but as you were there I couldn't deal with it in my usual way.'

'What would you have done if I hadn't been there?' Princess Margaret asked.

'Oh, I should have said a few well-chosen words.'

'Do tell me which words,' said the Princess with a merry twinkle in her eye.

And I replied, 'Good lord, I couldn't do that. You'd have me beheaded.'

She threw back her head and rocked with laughter. (It isn't what I say, it's how I say it.)

When I played a London club once, sitting in the audience was Lord Tennyson, the third baron, and he was out for fun. I was right in the middle of a long, favourite story of mine when he shouted, 'Nuts!' I carried on as though nothing had happened. At the end, when I took my bow, I said to the waiter, 'Have you given that gentleman his nuts?' The audience loved that.

It happened before the war. I was touring in an Army show some years later when a man came backstage to see me. His face was familiar, but I couldn't quite place him. 'Nuts,' he grinned, by way of introduction. It was Lord Tennyson again. He was followed by a soldier bearing a bottle of brandy and a crate of Bass which we drank to the last drop.

When I played the Waldorf Astoria – at the time of the Korean war – I discovered that American audiences joined in all the time. They were always shouting things and one had to be ready with comebacks. One Texan yelled loudly, 'Why don't you give Hong Kong to the Chinese Communists and appease *them*?'

'Would you mind not interrupting me when I am working,' I asked him. 'How would you like it if I came and kicked the broom out of your hands while you were working?'

I had a joke about an ugly woman which I used to slip in after things like that.

One night in a pub I saw the ugliest woman I've ever seen.

Not just ordinarily ugly, but really revolting. She had a parrot on her shoulder and as she walked up to the bar she said to the barman, 'Guess what I've got on my shoulder and I'll take you home to bed.' He said, 'An octopus?' She said, 'OK. That's good enough.'

I had just started this joke one night when an American woman stood up and waved an angry fist in my direction. 'Are you referring to me?' she shouted.

It was too good to be true. I couldn't believe my luck. It made me laugh so much I couldn't complete the joke that night. I often wondered whether she had been to see the show before and had decided to do that spot of ad-libbing.

Members of the Crazy Gang used to pop in to catch my night-club act in the West End after their Palladium show was over.

I appreciated their interruptions from the audience because they were so professional and funny that their exchanges enhanced my act. I wish I could remember some of the altercations. When other comedians tried it, things sometimes got out of hand. I remember one little fellow who often came to call out punchy things and made me uneasy. I was never sure whether he was being jovial or was secretly hoping to devastate my act.

I once heard that during a scene in a play in which he was touring Australia, an English actor had to walk to a table, lift up a cover and say, 'What have we got for breakfast?' 'Arseholes!' yelled a ribald Aussie voice from the audience. Without a pause, the actor continued, 'Apart from Australian delicacies, what have we got for breakfast?'

When I was appearing at Llandudno, I was heckled by a man in the audience as soon as I started my act. I chatted back to the heckler, but I could get no sense out of him. So I said to the audience, 'Shall I sling him out?' And everybody shouted, 'Yes!'

I jumped into the body of the kirk and said to the chap, 'This way, please.'

He got to his feet and I was most relieved to see that he

was quite a small man. I led him to the exit door, threw him out and got back on stage and continued my act.

I am only recounting this incident because Michael Bentine, who was also on the bill, was so impressed by how I had dealt with the disturbance that for ages afterwards he told the story wherever he went.

I don't know why Michael made such a song about it, actually, but his punchline was good. He recalled the heckler's indignant lament as he found himself in the street: 'I came especially to see Terry-Thomas – and he's chucked me out!'

I once interrupted somebody else's act because I hated the crude way she was treating her audience. Hollywood star Betty Hutton was appearing in a West End club and behaving badly. I was out front, taking the night off. Audience reaction had been cool.

'What's the matter with you?' Betty kept shouting at the tables. 'Don't you know how to clap?'

She went on and on in this vein.

I found her abrasive and eventually stood up and quietly suggested she got on with her act. There was loud applause – for me.

Betty Hutton turned to the band-leader and said, 'Who's that?'

The audience cheered and laughed. They thought it was terribly funny she didn't know who I was.

3   Titbits

It was at the Brighton Hippodrome where I slipped on a carpet onstage and fractured my right wrist. My new high-heeled shoes were the trouble. In that scene, I was masquerading as my wife's German maid. The wig I was wearing had been styled by Raymond (Mr Teasie Weasie) and my clothes designed by St John Roper. Suddenly – down I went, all fourteen stone of me. I had to carry on with my wrist in plaster. In drag, but certainly not limp-wristed.

I had shaved off my moustache for this part. I suppose I need not have done because quite a number of women wore them effectively.

Within five days of my fall, the play, Gilbert Wakefield's *Room for Two* (being revived after seventeen years) opened for a month's run at the Prince of Wales Theatre.

The critics were unimpressed by my first venture into farce. 'How unfunny for Terry-Thomas,' reported Cecil Wilson. Milton Shulman said in the *Evening Standard*: 'From the guffaws around me, I gathered that some of the audience found Mr Terry-Thomas in women's clothes mildly amusing. I merely report the fact. It would need a psychologist to explain it.' The *Daily Herald*'s Paul Holt wrote: 'I am sorry that Terry-Thomas who, after all, is a personality, should be submitted to this old-fashioned slush, made to wear wigs and gallivant in bathrooms.'

At least we lasted the month. Longer than my second 'straight role' project at the Duke of York's Theatre, five years later. That had such poor reviews that impresario Henry Sherek decided to withdraw the play after ten days. Adapted by Robin Maugham from Claude Magnier's *Oscar*, it was retitled *It's in the Bag*. I played a wealthy soap manufacturer who was blackmailed.

On the provincial tour, the audiences were rolling in the aisles and we had rave notices in Brighton, Edinburgh and Glasgow. But in London, the critics slammed it. John Mortimer wrote in the *Evening Standard*: 'I can't say that the play is made up for by the presence in it of Mr Terry-Thomas because he and the play are entirely separate matters ... [He] ... is a delightful and talented comedian ... as the soap manufacturer he is largely wasted, but he does give us a hilarious nervous breakdown and some lines he appeared to be adding, no doubt in desperation, to the script.'

Richard Briers, who is a second cousin of mine, had a small part in the play and was very good. As a boy he had come to visit me when I was in *Piccadilly Hayride*. Although he had given the impression of being about fifteen or sixteen, he can only actually have been thirteen years old. He puffed briskly at a succession of cigarettes, and told me over lunch at the Queen's in Leicester Square, that he had decided to become a comedian too.

'Hang on, do you know anything about the stage? And comedians?' I asked. 'For instance, where would you get your material?'

'I'll find it somewhere,' said Richard, cheerily.

So that he could pick up a tip or two, I sent him a collection of books about the theatre and actors including a favourite of mine about the life of John Henry Brodrib (who later became better known as Henry Irving).

Richard got a job in an electrical shop and later, a scholarship to RADA. With no nepotic help from me, he appeared in my film *A Matter of Who* (1961); and he was awful – which wasn't his fault. Later, I did ask for him to join me in my TV series, *The Old Campaigner*, in 1968, and he was as good as I knew he would be. I predict that Richard is in for really big things and by that, I mean exceptionally big.

I did not complete my hat-trick in a 'straight role' until more than one decade later, in Sydney, Australia, where I played the lead in a farce with an all-Australian cast.

At that time I was so popular 'down under' that a Sydney cinema ran a Terry-Thomas season of films to coincide with the run of the play.

We had full houses, I am happy to say, despite reviews like the following: 'Terry-Thomas is a very funny man, at the top of the tree as a movie comic. Affability and charm float from him in all directions.

'By all reports he doesn't need the money, so I am wondering what persuaded him to subject himself to the nightly game of starring in *Don't Just Lie There, Say Something*, on stage at the Metro Theatre.

'Harry M Miller must have dangled a particularly attractive carrot before him to engage in this indifferently scripted farce by Michael Pertwee.

'Terry-Thomas's brand of blithering idiocy, shining on the screen, is not so suited to the role of stage *farceur* where equal membership of a tight-knit acting team is the rule.

'The first-night impression he gave was of a gagging comedian hungry-eyed for audience approval, a man indulging his talent.

'But despite all the ego-tripping and game-playing, there was quite a lot to laugh at in this in-and-out-and-under-the-bed frolic, with scantily clad curvaceous popsies.

'For them, perhaps, being in company with the great man is compensation enough for taking part in such a fatuous affair.'

I shall always be grateful to the Australian drama critic for that one.

(Talking about Australia, I liked the tale of when Sir Noël Coward was in Sydney, in a lift, and someone said to him, 'Aren't you Noël Coward? Say something Australian.' And Sir Noël replied: 'Kangarooooooo!')

*

By the mid-Fifties my marriage had really floundered and Pat and I were living apart. In 1954 she had moved out of the flat into a place we called the Cowshed, just off Old Brompton Road. But she must have retained a key to the flat. On one spectacular occasion she returned.

She quietly let herself in, then charged upstairs. And surprised me with a vivacious blonde Australian singer called Lorrae Desmond who had popped by to pick up her passport, or something. She had been with a Forces' tour I had done in Kenya.

Pat took a dog's lead out of her bag and started thrashing Lorrae with it. For once she didn't shout, just stood there angrily lashing out with the leather lead.

With great presence of mind, considering that she was starkers, Lorrae did not let herself appear to be affected at all by this attack. She pulled the sheets up to her neck and started turning the pages of *The Observer*.

Eventually, Pat said, 'That's really taken the stuffing out of me. Have you a bottle of champagne?'

I found a bottle for her, and she left. The scene had lasted only a few minutes, but it was unnerving. It certainly took the stuffing out of *me*.

Pat never stopped reproaching herself for this action. Our marriage had been in tatters, but she was convinced that it was her outburst with the lead that finally split us. For ages afterwards, she told her friends that if she hadn't done that, we might have ridden our crisis, as we had others before, and got back together again.

The Press did not get wind of our break-up until 1957, three years after we had been apart. The *Daily Mail*'s perceptive and pithy columnist, Paul Tanfield, might not have found out even then, had I not been arrested at midnight, just before Christmas, and charged with driving a car while under the influence of drink.

During the filming of *Tom Thumb* at Elstree, that day, I had suffered a bad attack of lumbago, so I was feeling both tired and ill. I should have gone home to bed, but I had promised a friend to tell a few jokes at his firm's Christmas party in the Trocadero restaurant, and I didn't want to let him down.

When I arrived at the Trocadero, the commissionaire said, 'That's all right, Mr T. Leave the car to me.'

I got out of my 4½-litre olive-green Jensen drophead coupé and he drove it off. I went upstairs and did the show.

To cheer myself up at various times during the day, I had had a glass of beer, a brandy and ginger ale, two brandies and soda and a champagne cocktail. But I certainly wasn't what I call drunk – just ill – when I left the party. I had with me Lorrae Desmond's white Maltese terrier, Dinkum, to look after.

Two policeman were standing by my car in Great Windmill Street. One of them said, 'This car shouldn't be parked there. Move it on.'

When I tried to explain that I had not been responsible for parking it there, they were quite offhand. This made me see red and a few angry words were said. The moment I got into the car and started up the engine, one of the officers leaned inside, switched off the ignition and grabbed me. When he said, 'I am arresting you,' I replied, 'Don't be bloody silly.'

As the two of them led me through a small crowd of intrigued passers-by to a Black Maria in Piccadilly Circus, I realized what it must have been like for Oscar Wilde when he was taken to Reading gaol in broad daylight manacled to a policeman.

I was taken to West End Central police station and after undergoing various tests, they charged me.

I had tried to liven the proceedings with a few merry quips and at one point I – unwisely – joked to a police inspector, 'Be quiet. I am in charge here.' This line fell rather flat and I spent the rest of the night in a cell.

Next morning – Christmas Eve – at Bow Street, I was remanded on bail for three weeks in my own recognizance of £25.

It turned into a really unhappy Christmas when I found

that Dinkum the dog had disappeared from my car, which had been driven to the police station, in Savile Row, by my pianist, Jack Martin. Also missing was my beautiful black coat with a fur collar. A reward was put up for the return of the dog.

Lorrae Desmond, my secret steady girl-friend, was distraught. 'Dinkum means more to me than anyone I know in this country,' she wailed from Stockton-on-Tees where she was appearing in pantomine.

I felt awful about it. To save the dog the discomfort of having to spend long hours in Lorrae's dressing-room while she did the panto, I had offered to keep him with me in London. 'Don't worry, darling, he'll be quite safe with me,' I had assured her. Now he was lost.

Dinkum was the first part of this incredible tale to have a happy ending. He reappeared a few days later. A chap called Ron Sterry delivered him and said, 'A couple of fellows brought him round to me and asked me to return him.'

Lorrae was overjoyed and drove straight down from Stockton-on-Tees for a tearful reunion with Dinks who, the *Daily Mail* informed its readers, 'had made eight TV appearances'.

Next day, having put two and two together by making a few enquiries, the *Mail*'s heading read: 'Terry-Thomases are living apart.'

In January I pleaded not guilty and elected to go for trial. My bail was renewed.

Two weeks later I was presented to the Queen Mother at the Royal Film Performance of Alec Guinness's *The Horse's Mouth*, at the Empire, Leicester Square. Lauren Bacall and Maurice Chevalier were among the other stars on the receiving line, so that event brightened up my February a bit. Even though I knew I was not guilty, it was not nice to have a drunken driving charge hanging over me. Whenever I went into a pub people grinned, looked knowing and wagged their fingers. It seemed I had publicly been judged and found guilty before I'd even got to the London Sessions.

I felt that even more when my application to join the RAC was turned down. All this time my lumbago had been killing me. A friend suggested that if I were to join the famous motorists' club in Pall Mall, I should be able to use the Turkish baths there and, hopefully, do my back some good. But I was blackballed. It was worse than being turned down by a tart in Piccadilly.

William Hickey, the *Daily Express* columnist, went to the club and put into print what a lot of people had – rightly or wrongly – deduced. 'In the bar yesterday,' wrote Hickey, 'there was a certain feeling against the Committee for refusing the application. Members thought it might be taken as pre-judging his court case.'

A couple of days after that, a jury at the London Sessions took just twenty-three minutes to find me not guilty. They had heard about my lumbago and the extremely arduous work I was doing on *Tom Thumb*. A still from the film was produced in evidence on my behalf.

I mentioned my perpetual dry mouth and the sore eyes I suffered on that Gothic set caused by the dust that was sprayed over the cobwebs. 'Not real cobwebs, of course,' I told the court, helpfully. 'We can't get spiders to work for us.'

When asked why I had told the police inspector at the station to be quiet, I explained that I was just joking. The prosecution then wanted to know if I thought that that had been the time and place to exercise my sense of humour.

'That is a strange question to put to a comedian,' I said. 'He has a different attitude to life from an average person.'

I wonder what I would have replied if the judge or prosecuting counsel had asked me then: 'Would you apply this line of reasoning to a murder trial?'

My counsel had decided that he would not call any witnesses, though several were in court. On one occasion, when referring to a nurse who had given me some pills on the morning of the incident, he said, 'Is this lady here in court?' 'Yes,' I replied. 'Would you point her out?' And I did. 'Would you stand up?' And she stood up. I wanted to wave to her and say, 'It's jolly nice of you to come along.' She was the nurse at Elstree MGM studios and charming.

At any rate, my lawyer had decided that he was not going to call any of these witnesses unless it was absolutely necessary on the assumption that if you did not call witnesses, you got the last word. My considered opinion, after limited experience, made me think that this was not really worth while because it was the judge who always got the last word in the summing up.

The prosecution had got the bit firmly between his teeth. 'Why?' said he, gripping his right lapel, just as they did on the flicks, 'Why have none of these people who could speak for you been called? Your pianist, Jack Martin, for instance. Jack Martin. Is he dead?'

I said, 'No, he's not dead, he's very much alive. As a matter of fact, he is here today, although he is in pretty ropy condition. He has a broken leg.'

And counsel for the prosecution said, like the good feed he was, 'Ah, so he's alive?' To which I replied, on cue, 'Yes, but not kicking.'

This, as far as I can remember, was the only time that there was laughter in court.

*

Lorrae Desmond spent about ten years in the UK and for most of that time we were inseparable. She was jolly, always joking and very exciting to be with. She brimmed over with enthusiasm. One of the things that first attracted me to her, apart from her being the sexiest person I had ever met, was that she had trained as a straight singer. When she appeared with me in a 1956 TV series called *Strictly T-T*, the *Radio Times* described her as 'a sensational soprano ... a pop singer with brains'.

She was, and still is, wonderfully attractive, indeed, physically speaking, she was the greatest love of my life.

Never since have I met a more dedicated woman in bed. I would have married her like a shot, and we often discussed it, but Pat repeatedly refused to divorce me.

Lorrae and I loved travelling. Once, after I'd fallen from a horse, we flew to Madeira specifically to get my broken wrist working again. The chap at Guy's Hospital, who had set it, had warned me the wrist might never get right. But I knew that sea-water could do wonders and I was convinced that swimming would do the trick.

Lorrae was beside me, looking stunning and encouraging in a bikini, when the first big waves came towards me. Initially, I was petrified, because I could not use the right arm at all. But as each day passed, I could feel the arm getting stronger and stronger because Lorrae and I spent hours together in the water. When we got back to London, I had proved the medico wrong. My wrist was fine.

Other times we holidayed in Positano, Ischia, the South of France, Majorca …

In Capri we spent a lot of time with Valerie Hobson and MP John Profumo (who had yet to give his name to the famous 'affair'.) And on the Suez Canal, we bumped into Tessie O'Shea trying, in vain, to prevent her nose from burning by covering it with an hibiscus leaf.

On one trip to the South of France, we ducked off to a café and had a wonderful night listening to Stefan Grapelli. Afterwards, Stefan joined us at our table and I asked, 'How's it going?'

'It's all right,' he said, 'but our drummer has been sent to prison for rape.' I said, 'That's a bit of bad luck. What do you do about a drummer, then?' 'Oh, it's all worked out well,' said Stefan. 'One of the prison officers brings him down to play, every evening, and picks him up after the show.'

I also met Pablo Picasso in the South of France. I was invited to call at his home which had masses of bougainvillea of all colours around it. Picasso was all polished up, ready to go out. He had on the most delightful clothes: black velvet coat, black and grey houndstooth trousers, a pink shirt made of Irish linen and a green scarab to fasten the shirt.

We didn't talk about his pictures but the ashtrays he had just started designing. I asked him, 'Is it true that somebody once said to you, "Can I have a word in your eye?"' He didn't think it a bit funny.

Once, in the South of France, I was a guest of another artist, John Spencer Churchill and his wife. It was a formal day until the coffee was served. Then suddenly, John and I found ourselves fighting over nothing. We went upstairs and we went downstairs and smashed a lot of crockery and glass and things on the way. I think John's wife, not to mention the staff, was a bit worried. But there was no blood, just a few scratches. Eventually, we both sank down exhausted, unable to move. As I sat there, getting my breath back, I was very much smitten by a mural of the Last Supper, painted by John, depicting everybody as monkeys.

Before we finally married other people, Lorrae had paid me a visit in Hollywood, where I was now a film-actor, and I had gone to see her 'down under'. In Sydney, we had one of our frequent tiffs. I was upset about something and in a rotten mood. I dropped Lorrae at a club and told the taxi-driver to take me back to where I was staying. The driver, who had heard me say goodnight to this vivacious blonde, asked me, 'Could you have gone to bed with her?' 'I could have,' I said, 'if I had tried very hard.'

He then asked me, 'Are you English?' When I nodded, he said, 'I thought there must be *something* wrong with you.'

Lorrae worked with me often, both on tour and in cabaret. This was easy to arrange as they were all my bills. But we fought like mad. I wanted to keep our friendship secret and she didn't think it necessary. For example, she would call loudly to a porter in a crowded hotel lobby, 'Harry, take my bags to Terry-Thomas's room.' (Not even *Mr!*)

Most of our fights were based on nothing and were frequently conducted on long distance telephones. The positively throbbing reconciliations that followed made every little squabble worth while. Work was always moving us in different directions; perhaps the partings kept our romance alive.

I don't know whether I was Lorrae's only fellow; I have a feeling I was. But I had other girl-friends. It is quite extraordinary when I think how many there were. I recall one girl with a marvellous figure and a fabulous sports car. Highly glamorous she was. *And most gymnastic!*

In Sydney, a marvellously attractive coloured woman gave me the full treatment under a table. And a similar thing happened in a club in Bond Street. The girl, a pale blonde, told me that her husband was always nagging her that she was under-sexed. She set out to prove to me that she wasn't. She proved it all right! I should have given her husband a crate of champagne for having goaded her.

People who repeat what they say get on my nerves, but there was one voluptuous exception. She was a nice, bright starlet whom I took with me to Gibraltar when I made a film called *Operation Snatch*. She made a point of jumping into bed on top of me and shouting in a loud voice, over and over again, 'Happiness! Happiness!' Everyone on that film-set lusted after her. I was the envy of Gibraltar.

Until the 1950s girls could be topless on stage only as long as they didn't move. I successfully disregarded this by-law in variety theatres and clubs around the country. I had a girl stooge called Bunty Darling who gradually stripped as I conducted a mock auction. First she took off her shirt. Then half of her bra revealing one beautiful, pink orb. Then the other. Eventually, as I reached the going-going-gone bit, she reached to rip off her panties – and we blacked out. Bunty suffered no inhibitions at all. I'd had no problems getting her to do the act with me. She was what one might loosely term a statuesque girl. Seven girls had applied for the job. Competition had been keen. I enjoyed the auditioning immensely.

I became quite an authority on boobs. They seemed to be everywhere. Once, I had to do a photo-feature for *Picture Post* with Sabrina, whose only claim to fame were her magnificent breasts. Over lunch, the editor, Freddie Mullally, asked Sabrina if she could cook and she said she couldn't. 'Well darling,' said Freddie, 'I advise you to start learning.'

Lowering his gaze to a central point between her shoulders, he said, 'It won't be long before those two beauties of yours will have lost some of their glamour and resilience. And they'll no longer get you very far. Certainly not as far as a couple of good, well-cooked steaks.'

The day I saw Marilyn Monroe close to, I was disappointed, for she seemed almost ugly. Her hair was lank, she was wishy-washy, pale and not in very good shape. Probably she was very ill. I was reminded of a cheap, pink balloon, half blown-up. She didn't excite me and I wasn't at all impressed by her boobs.

Jayne Mansfield's were much better. When we made *A Guide for the Married Man* (1967) I saw everything she had through a diaphanous pink négligé she wore in a bedroom scene with me. She was in control of *her* boobs and presented them well. They weren't flabby, indeed, they were well-shaped and firm. As I've always said, packaging is everything.

I also made a film with Gina Lollobrigida and didn't find her as big-bosomed as I had been led to suppose, but then I tended to be a trifle greedy. Diana Dors was the same: fabulous figure but modest mammaries.

There's a nice tit-bit that her friends tell about actress Coral Browne. (I made two *Dr Phibes* films with her husband, Vincent Price.)

Coral went into a smart shop in Piccadilly, picked up a bra and asked, 'How much is this?' And the girl assistant said, 'Eight guineas.' Coral dropped the bra as if she had been stung. 'Eight guineas?' she echoed, 'I'd rather have them cut off.'

There was another large-bosomed girl – Nadiuska – who sticks prominently in my mind. I made a film called *Spanish Fly* with her and Leslie Phillips, on the island of Minorca.

In one scene I had to pull this terribly attractive actress from the drink and neither Nadiuska nor anyone else had told me she would be stark naked. But I reacted very well. 'By jove!' I said, 'How lovely! Come this way.' I was enjoying it so much I deliberately fluffed the lines so that we had to do the scene three or four times.

I was once sitting on the edge of the stage of the Eve Club, in Regent Street, watching Lorrae Desmond perform, when a complete stranger at the next table remarked, 'That singer has got the most beautiful bosoms.'

'Do you really think so?' I said, turning, as Lorrae's number finished. 'Thank you – I'll tell her.'

'Don't go yet,' said the chap, 'Give her a chance to get her clothes off.'

I have always been a keen writer of comedy and since my youth have had ambitions to write a book on sex – which is humour of a different sort.

I remember my friend, John Barnes, telling me: 'You're flogging a dead horse, dear boy. Do you honestly think that you know enough about it to write a guide-book to sex?'

I read out my first tip to John: 'Always have an extra pillow handy. This can be slipped under the lady's bottom at the appropriate moment and will permit even closer contact.'

Really, with a lot more practical little tips like that one, I still feel that it would be a book with a good chance of being successful. I might get on with that book when I've finished this one.

A famous American singer must have heard of my planned sex-manual. When we worked together once, she said to me, 'Before I knew you, Terry, I was afraid you would be a sex maniac. Now I'm afraid that you're not.'

Knowledgeable as I was on the subject of deep-bosomed women, I was considered even more of an expert on clothes. Not just fancy waistcoats. I spent a lot of time, and a great deal of money, on building and maintaining my image as a natty dresser.

My formal clothes came from Cyril Castle and my riding gear from Huntsman, both Savile Row establishments. Mr Castle made me two-piece suits to complement my fancy waistcoats and I had about twenty-four suits which I wore on a rotating basis. One of the features I demanded was a breast-pocket seven inches deep to accommodate my cigarette holder. My lapel buttonholes had to be specially designed too, so that a clove carnation would fit easily. The carnation had to be clove. I got mine from a florist in Old Brompton Road and never pinned them into place. That wasn't – and isn't – done. They had to fit snugly into the buttonhole. Wherever I went, a clove carnation adorned me. Even if I only slipped out to the pub, I always dressed as if I were going to a stage or a cabaret floor.

In February 1953 came the highest accolade. In the *Tailor and Cutter*'s list of the Top Ten Best-Dressed Men, I was placed first. The other nine were: Sir Malcolm Sargent, John Mills, Sir William Darling, Sir Frederick Browning, Earl Alexander, Douglas Fairbanks, Cecil Beaton, Terence Rattigan and Prince Charles (noted: 'his baby bow tie and junior deerstalker').

To get into the list had meant a hell of a lot of work. To keep in, a hell of a lot more. One could never let up. I was fortunate in having a housekeeper who took pride in cleaning and pressing my clothes to ensure I would always be immaculate. She was Gladys Cooper's sister. She had given up acting on the stage because – she used to explain – as soon as she came on, people in the audience would whisper, 'That's Gladys Cooper's Sister'. as though that were her name. It sounded just as though she was being hissed. I can't remember what she was called ... oh yes: Gladys Cooper's Sister, of course.

My image of dandyism became so much a part of me, no self-respecting journalist missed the opportunity of describing my outfits.

A few examples: 18 April 1949: 'Terry-Thomas, in brown bowler hat, drove actress, Hy Hazel, round Hyde Park in a pony and trap.'

7 June 1952: 'Terry-Thomas must be given much of the credit for the return of the flowered waistcoat.'

4 June 1956: 'During Derby Week, Terry-Thomas was noticed on a fine chestnut doing a neat trot through Hyde Park. He was immaculately dressed in close-fitting fawn trousers with instep-strap, long-waisted black jacket, fawn shirt, black and white check tie ... practically a male fashion plate of the 1850s except that he had no stove-pipe hat.'

In *Reynolds News*, November 1959, I was quoted: 'I am a dandy – or rather, a damdy. I don't dress conventionally and I'm damned if I ever will. Dress should be attractive. How many who ride in Rotten Row with the full regalia are not so attractive as they might be, say, in leather jeans and a black, silk shirt?'

Time, 25 June 1965, wrote: 'On his travels, like any blimp setting off on safari, he packs his portmanteaus (sic) with sartorial accoutrements for every conceivable occasion: white flannels for tennis, plus fours for golf, blazer for cricket, bowler, boater and deerstalker, tweeds, pinstripes, tails. Everything but the old elephant gun.

'He claims that he needs all those togs for professional use, but off-stage, he is seldom seen wearing the wrong suit or the same suit twice.'

Even when I was arrested on that drunken driving charge, the sartorial note crept into the *Daily Express* report of that night: 'Terry-Thomas was wearing a purple-coloured smoking jacket with soft, turned-down collar, black bow-tie and overcoat.'

Later, for my hearing at the London Sessions, the *Daily Telegraph* noted: 'He wore a curly-brim bowler, dark suit and coat and waistcoat of the same dark-red colour as the carnation in his lapel.'

Thomas Wiseman, in an article headed: 'The Dandy on Horseback' wrote in the *Evening Standard*, in April 1955: 'Terry-Thomas enjoys a reputation as one of our leading comics.

'He can afford to indulge his taste for elegance (he owns

80 suits, 22 dinner jackets and tail-suits, 150 fancy waist-coats), he can employ a valet, a chauffeur, a secretary, a personal publicist; he can run two cars, does not have to offend the palate by drinking anything other than the best wines. He is able to participate in the "millionaires' sport" of fox-hunting and keeps two horses.'

With that sort of thing being written about me, no wonder the men at the Inland Revenue took notice. They wanted to know if I resold my suits.

I sent this letter to *The Times*, on 16 February 1957:

> Sir, Inspectors of Taxes have acquired a reputation for wanting not only the greater part of one's income, but also the very clothes off one's back. I thought, until today, that this reputation was quite undeserved and indeed, that it was probably the invention of some low, music-hall comedian. I am now told by my accountant, who is professionally impeccable, that my own Tax Inspector now wishes to know whether I sell my old suits. Unbelievable, isn't it? I wonder if they ask deep-sea divers the same question?'

This brought a reply headed, 'A Taxing Question', three days later:

> In his letter of 16 February, Mr Terry-Thomas does his Inspector of Taxes less than justice. My own Inspector does not inquire whether I sell my old clothes, perhaps because I am still wearing them, but more likely because I get no tax concession on those I buy. No doubt Mr Terry-Thomas, by virtue of his profession, needs to spend £X a year on new clothes and is allowed to deduct their cost from his gross income. Why therefore, if he sells such clothes later for £Y, should he not be limited to tax relief on £X - £Y only? I support the Inspector. HR Murray Shaw, 35 Viceroy Close, Bristol Road, Birmingham 5.

I had to put pen to paper again in *The Times* of 22 February:

Sir, Do forgive me for reopening the wardrobe door, but I do not sell my old clothes and have no intention – at present – of entering this ancient and honourable trade. If I did have any old clothes that I did not want to wear, I should follow my mother's excellent example and swap them for an aspidistra or perhaps, a goldfish. This raises another interesting point: what percentage of the aspidistra or the goldfish would be claimed by the Tax Inspector?

(I used to tell a story about a tailor who had a very measly trick played on him by one of those awful leg-puller chaps who went into his shop and said, 'I want you to make me a suit out of green billiard-table cloth, eight buttons, double-breasted and leopard-skin collar and cuffs. And I want it ready by next Thursday.'

Thursday came, but the man did not and as each day passed, it became increasingly obvious that the man was not going to collect the suit. The tailor decided to go away for a few days' holiday to get over his annoyance that was giving him ulcers.

He told his boy assistant, 'Look after the shop.' And just as he was leaving, he said, 'Oh yes. One other thing, I want you to sell that bloody suit. Cheerio.' And off he went.

When he returned, a few days later, he asked, 'How did things go?'

'Oh, everything's fine, Guv'nor.'

'I suppose you didn't sell that green suit?'

'Oh yes, I sold it. Got forty-eight quid for it.'

'You didn't!' said the tailor.

'Yes, I certainly did.'

'Well, what did the man say? He must have said something.'

'No,' said the boy, 'he didn't. Not a word. But his

guide-dog did growl a bit.')

Hand in hand with my image as a fashion plate, went my reputation as an authority on snobbery. So when Foyles gave a luncheon to launch the Duke of Bedford's *Book of Snobs*, it was natural that I was asked to speak. And when London University debated the motion: 'A gentleman has no part to play in modern society', I was invited, with David Frost, to give my views.

I regarded Rex Harrison as an example of an extremely snooty person. If he didn't think that you were in his class, he would ignore you. Once, when I flew to Florence, I noticed that the actor (whose real name was Reginald Carey) and his current wife were fellow passengers.

Mrs Harrison smiled at me and whispered to Reg, 'That's Terry-Thomas.' But Reg wasn't having any. He kept his eyes deliberately averted. I amused myself by seeing whether or not I could make him smile. I couldn't. It was a silly situation because the first-class compartment was so small that it was impossible not to notice somebody. What's more, Reg and I had spent quite a bit of time together in the past, in other people's houses, so it wasn't as if we were strangers.

At the time when the differences between U and Non-U were being discussed, the *Daily Express* ran a 'Guide to U in the Professions'. I was their automatic choice as 'The father of "U" in Show Biz'. 'U is my heart's delight,' I told them, and went on, I'm afraid, at some length....

'You can usually spot a U comedian as he is ruled by a code of speech and behaviour which makes any brigade of guards seem a very shoddy shower indeed. You can recognize him by the way he dresses. He avoids, whenever possible, wearing a felt hat with a dinner jacket and indeed, rarely wears a dinner jacket, as this prevents him from wearing his old school tie. He therefore usually wears a double-breasted blazer which also gives him a chance to show his regimental buttons and crest. If, by any chance, the occasion makes a dinner jacket essential, for instance, if he condescends to appear at a Royal Variety Performance, he avoids a made-up bow-tie, always tying his own, double-ended. This might appear to be pointless as you can't possibly tell the difference between a ready-made bow-tie and a self-tied one since the buckle is concealed under the collar. But it simply isn't done, and besides, after seven or eight years, the buckle is liable to corrode.

'A U comedian never refers to footlights, but to "floats", and curtains are known as "tabs". The musical director is referred to as Charlie, but a U comedian would no more think of talking to a musical director from the stage than he would think of singing in tune, or for that matter, singing at all. If he does sing, it is more said than sung, rather like Noël Coward rehearsing.

'A U comedian (not comic) never begins his act by saying, "A funny thing happened to me as I was walking to the theatre today", although it might be permissible to say, "A rather droll thing happened to me as I was motoring to the theatre today". (A U comedian does not walk.) Neither does he refer to his relatives, however distant, unless of course they are titled.

'If he does by any chance refer to his wife, he never calls her, "the wife", "my lady wife", "my good lady", "the missus", "the old woman" or "the ball and chain" but "the memsahib". He never uses a feed, but occasionally a straight man – that is, somebody to whom he can be rude. If he uses a chauffeur-cum-valet-cum-pianist he sees that he is suitably garbed for each occasion; e.g. socks are always worn at the piano.

'By now you will not be surprised to hear that there are very few U comedians in the U class, or as we say, in the U boat. As far as I know there's only one.'

I could have added, 'You don't say serviette, but table napkin. And you don't have a mascot, nodding dog or any other doll on the back window of your motor car (never "car"), although if you do hang a dangler from the window, you are doing the public a good service. You are informing other motorists that the man who is driving is an idiot.

Nobody but an idiot would have a dangler in his car.'

By this stage in my career, it will be only too obvious to you, Dear Reader, that I had become disgustingly sure of myself. Perhaps Robert Graves, the poet, had the right idea by literally bringing me down to earth. When I called on the great man in Majorca, I anticipated an intellectual conversation about Greek mythology. The only thing Graves would discuss with me was compost. He tramped me round his garden, stuck forks into things and made me smell it close. *Merde*!

Another time I was brought up short was when I paid a visit to a friend of my father in Paris. I arrived in this very soignée house and was introduced to this man sitting in an armchair, with a dog at his feet.

When coffee was brought in, he took some of his, poured it into the saucer and stirred it with his thumb. Not knowing whether it was the thing to do or not, I thought I had better be on the safe side, so I followed suit, stirring the sugar in as well.

What a fool I felt when he bent down to give his to the dog.

I have gone through a lot of money in my life. Millions ... yes millions, of pounds, not to mention francs, much of it just squandered and wasted. But I have invariably done well out of my investments. I have always had a fairly good feeling as to what should be done on the stock market, and it normally came off.

I was talked into one of my first investments by my chauffeur at the time, a chap called Bray. Eventually, I had to get rid of him because he was interfering too much in my life. He would come and talk money matters at the most inopportune moments, such as when I was getting ready for a performance, or going over my script. One day he caught me in a receptive mood and persuaded me to invest in a general store, on the outskirts of Putney, with his wife, Betty.

I bought the Munster Road Food Stores and gave Betty the

place to run, plus a certain amount of capital. I kept in the background, changed the name of the store to Betty's and wrote letters, signed by Betty, to be popped into letter-boxes up and down Munster Road. We did very well.

Came the day when the responsibility of owning a successful general store began to worry me. There were quite enough headaches in show business. I didn't need more. I decided to get out of Provisions.

I suggested to Betty that – now she was on her feet – she might care to buy the store from me. She pleaded lack of means. All my associates, agents and solicitors told me there was absolutely nothing I could do. They pointed out it did not suit anyone to pay money for a shop if they could get it for nothing.

I had to do a bit of logical thinking.

I told her, 'Betty, I've decided to close the store.' 'You can't do that,' she said, aghast. And I said, 'Yes I can. I'd like to have the key tomorrow evening.'

She paid up. I got the money and she kept the business.

I was not so shrewd when it came to producing films. I have gone into several ventures without success.

I once formed a film company called Tomkin with a friend, Douglas Rankin. We planned a series of travelogues to be shown in the cinema as supports. The first one was called *Terry-Thomas in Tuscany*.

We had a team of a dozen or so people and I imagined that as I was a performer myself, I should get a hell of a lot of faithful support from the team, but it was not so. For some extraordinary reason that I could never understand, everybody was always out to do the producer of any film whoever he was. I had to be on the watch the whole time.

When it came to my scene in *Tuscany*, I couldn't get away from London, so we decided to do it on Hampstead Heath. We figured we would shoot it so artfully that nobody would be able to tell it wasn't Tuscany. Then I saw the camera chaps loading their gear. 'What's up?' I asked. 'We're going home. There's not enough light.' 'What do you mean?' I said. 'This is glorious light.'

I found the first assistant and he set up a scene outside a restaurant where people were eating. We hung a few bottles of Chianti around for the authentic Italian touch and photographed it in the beautiful pink rays of the setting sun.

It turned out as good as anything in the film. I bet more than one person felt nostalgic for Pisa when they saw our dastardly clever bits done on Hampstead Heath.

But, of course, to finish the film, eventually we did have to go to Italy where, in one sequence, I interviewed Emilio Pucci, the designer, one of the few men, in my opinion, to have achieved a rare combination: to be delightfully flamboyant in a very dignified way.

We also filmed artist Annigoni in his studio in Florence. This was during the period when he was totally immersed in the task of buying back as many of his own paintings as he could. He seemed quite besotted by the project and already his studio, which was curiously dark, appeared to be packed with canvases.

When the film was shown in a 'full supporting programme' at the Odeon, Leicester Square, I mingled with the crowds as they left.

I heard one chap say, 'That was number one in the series and I liked it. I must look out for the next one.'

We made a little money out of *Tuscany*, but not much.

Second in the series *Terry-Thomas in the South of France (Iles de Hyère)* was shot largely on the Ile de Levant, a nudist island. We had to go through the motions of getting permits, but there was no opposition. Not one naturist objected to being filmed. As our camera rolled, they all carried on posing in the water trying hard to look natural. They certainly didn't succeed. I found them a pretty unhealthy, shapeless and uninspiring lot. In fact, I didn't consider we had got anything on film worth the journey.

We didn't make any money on that one.

Last of the series *Terry-Thomas in Northern Ireland* was the most disastrous. We filmed a lot of drunks. One was a man who was so sloshed he had no control over his legs. We kept standing him up but the moment we let him go he slowly fell backwards like a sack of potatoes and his legs bounced off the ground like a puppet's. He hadn't a clue as to what was going on.

The series took a year to film. An interesting experience, but Douglas Rankin, a nice chap and all that, was not the ideal partner if you wanted to make money. He didn't take things seriously at all.

I was never able to cure myself completely of film producing. In the last two years I have invested money in three films of which, to date, I have made a loss of one hundred per cent.

They were made as supporting features or television spots but I don't think any of them have been seen anywhere yet.

One was about Tannit, the legendary goddess of the island of Ibiza. Tannit was played by a large, rather abrasive black girl and several midgets, imported from the Spanish mainland, were cast in other roles.

My French director certainly had some way-out ideas about goddesses.

4   To Be or Not to Be ... Funny

At Jack Lemmon's wedding party, I told Groucho Marx a joke. I thought he would like it, and he did. 'Great! Now I want you to tell that same joke to Jack over there,' he said. I thought he meant the bridegroom, but it wasn't jovial Jack Lemmon who Groucho had in mind. It was Jack Benny who was coming towards us with his usual unsmiling face. I was positively thrilled. I had always been a fan of Jack Benny.

Groucho said, 'This is Terry-Thomas and he's just told me a very funny story that I'm sure will tickle you to death, Jack. It's especially interesting for you because it's about a violin player. Off you go, Terry.'

So I told this story. There was a man who for years had had a recurring dream that he could play the violin beautifully. One day he saw a violin in a shop window in Bond Street, went in and asked, 'How much is that?' The chap inside said, 'This is a remarkably fine violin. In fact, it's a Stradivarius – which is Italian for violin.'

The man bought it, dashed round the corner, sat in a square and started to play. Fantastic. His dream had come true. He really could play and never had a lesson in his life. But it wasn't long before he was booked by a policeman for causing an obstruction.

So he went to Africa. While in the jungle, he decided to play the violin again, this time to the animals. All the animals of the forest crept up, surrounded him and listened in rapt enjoyment. Not a sound could be heard.

Then a very old lion arrived. He took in the scene and then leapt at the violinist and tore him to pieces.

A young leopard remarked indignantly, 'What on earth did you do that for? There was this man playing lovely music. We were all enjoying it. And now you've gone and spoilt it.'

The old lion cupped a paw behind his ear, put his head close to the leopard and said, 'Eh?'

Jack Benny gave me a polite half-smile and said, 'Thank you. I'll see you a little bit later.'

In other words: Don't ring me. I'll call you.

Getting me to tell him that story was typical of Groucho Marx's humour. He knew that Jack Benny wouldn't enjoy it because when I got to know Jack well, I discovered that he was a man with very little sense of humour, which shattered me because I was such a fan of his.

When Jack Benny died, I was invited to take over his TV show. His team of writers came to my apartment in the Beverly Hills Hotel to read the script they had written for me. At the end, one of the writers asked, 'Don't you think it's funny?' So I said, 'No, I don't!' Another writer wailed, 'You didn't laugh even once.'

It was a sad business altogether because the idea of my taking over the show fell flat after that and fizzled out. They wanted me to do Benny's material, which was damned silly. He had his style. I had mine.

What is the formula for raising laughs? That is something which varies from person to person. It's a matter of attack, timing, the reaction received, plus a few more mysterious ingredients – like confidence and charisma, to name two.

I was a comedy-actor but regarded myself, first and foremost, as a comedian with a built-in ability to inject humour into situations.

I spent an enormous amount of time studying how to write humour and reading books on the philosophical approach to it, but it didn't get me very far. I decided that humour was like a good watch. It would go well if left to do its job but the moment one started poking around, it went wonky.

So what I attempted to do was to have one gag running to another in order to make one long story. That saved a lot of time building up atmosphere.

The task of finding stories to tell was extremely difficult. It never stopped. I had several people helping me to find gags. My father passed on the ones he picked up from his golf club, the North Middlesex. He met lots of entertainers playing golf.

Another source was an uncle of Sid Field. He was a marvellous old man, as ancient as Balaclava, who had been on the variety stage as a stooge for over sixty years. He remembered many old comedians going back to Dan Leno and beyond and provided me with lots of stories I could use.

Dickie Henderson's father told the most unsophisticated stories. He said things like, 'My wife eats so much fish that her belly goes in and out with the tide.'

To me it was embarrassingly awful. Nobody could persuade me that anyone using that sort of material was worth listening to.

Arthur Askey was always Arthur Askey whether doing his act, playing dame or appearing with other people in sketches. He was a charming person and easy to work with. He once expressed his admiration for a joke of mine. 'I don't know how you get them. They're always new ones,' he said.

And I told him, 'No they're not. A lot of them come from my father's golf club.' Arthur said, 'What a pity my father doesn't play golf.'

The gag he liked especially was about the MP who won his seat by one vote and told the crowd, 'I came here as a stranger. I saw you. I fell in love with you. I wooed you. We became engaged. And now we are married.'

A voice came from the back: 'And I know what you are going to do to us now.'

Dancing a somewhat eccentric tango with the smashing
Joyce Grenfell on the set of *Blue Murder at St Trinians,* 1957.
(*Cinema Bookshop*)

What a handsome trio! Myself, Joyce Grenfell and Lionel
Jeffries relaxing on the set of *Blue Murder at St Trinians*.
(*Cinema Bookshop*)

Until the day she died, at 80, Pat wore a
silver locket that I had given her as an
early wedding anniversary gift with our
pictures inside.

It's not often that this happens at the dinner table! Peter Sellers, myself, Thorley Walters, Julie Hopkins and the lovely Kathryn Keeton on the set of *Carleton Browne of the FO*, 1958. (*Cinema Bookshop*)

Pat had this studio portrait taken to send to our friends just after our divorce. Archie, the dog, was my present to her. She called him her 'consolation prize'.

We both had a penchant for dressing up!

I realized early on that vulgarity had a part to play in comedy. Part of me loathed that and part of me loved it. For although the public adored blue material, like so many exciting things, it was dangerous. Max Miller, for instance. He was famed for his blue humour and it cost him money. Once, George Black fined him – I think it was £500 – for slipping in some filthy joke that had not been in the script. Black always demanded to see a copy of comedians' scripts and censored material if it was too near the knuckle. He felt he was entitled to do this because all performances had to be licensed by the Lord Chamberlain in any case and if the Lord Chamberlain decided to move in, it was Black who was jumped on first.

When comedians met while changing trains at Crewe station on Sunday mornings, the problem of blue jokes was constantly being discussed.

I was censored when I broadcast in *Variety Bandbox*. This is the story I wanted to tell on the programme.

There were two men in a bar and one of them said to the other, 'See that man over there. That's the 'ead master of 'arrer (Harrow).' The other man said, 'Who told you?' And the first one said, 'No one told me. I saw his picture in the paper. I'll tell you what I'll do. I'll go and ask him and if I'm right, you buy me a pint of beer. Right?' 'OK' the other man said.

So the chap walked over to the man, who was very soberly dressed in a black jacket and striped trousers, and he said, 'Excuse me, Sir. I've just had a bet with a pal of mine. I said you're the 'ead of 'arrer. Is that right?'

And the man put his glass of beer down very carefully on the bar and said, 'If you don't get out of here, I'll poke my finger in your eye. Slope off!'

So the chap went back to his pal who asked, 'Was 'e?' And the other one said, 'I don't know. He wouldn't say.'

At rehearsal, the producer, Joy Russell-Smith snapped, 'You can't possibly use that.' I asked, 'What's wrong with it?' And Joy said, 'You know perfectly well that the word "poke" is rude.'

I'm sorry to say that I didn't win on this one because I hadn't the patience. But when I recovered sufficiently from shock, I asked Joy, 'What do you do when you get a sentence like "Will you please poke the fire?"'

From Ronald Frankau, a most sophisticated comedian, I learned that one could be subtle and suggestive with humour and put it across without handing it to the audience on a plate. Yet Frankau was also fined for being too blue.

Sir Laurence Olivier considered that one of the best rôles he ever played was Archie Rice in *The Entertainer*. But I didn't rate it highly because – I couldn't accept the dialogue. It was not variety, nothing like it. No variety comedian ever used material quite as subtle as John Osborne wrote for Archie.

Comedians are not happy people. They all suffer from the blues. That is how you can tell a genuine comedian; he is frequently down in the dumps. There are many theories as to this. One that I subscribe to is that too much dabbling with laughter unbalances your life.

A lot of famous funny-men are undoubtedly unbalanced. I'm one! If you spend your life trying to make people laugh, you're bound to get a bit fed-up when they don't. As a general rule, most of the chaps who became comedians did so because, like me, they needed to draw attention to themselves.

When I made my doctor-prescribed début at the health farm near Tring, after *Piccadilly Hayride* ended, I was on the verge of a nervous breakdown. Overwork! Very often, since then, I have teetered on the borders of depression and melancholy. Each time I got better and thought I had depression beaten. Then it surged up again – and I'd go back to Tring in search of peace. Almost a regular visitor.

I have always chosen to attack my melancholia by running away from people. For when I'm in the abyss of depression, nothing seems good. I don't think I'm clever. And I certainly don't think I'm funny. In America I was once quoted as saying that it was up to every artiste to cosset his charisma as often as possible – whether he had charisma or not! You had to tell yourself constantly how clever you were.

I am sure there must be some comedians who are not megalomaniacs – the ones you never hear of! It is such a difficult profession in which to make your way that only the most egotistical can possibly survive. A comedian is on his own. While an actor can always claim that he is merely interpreting his author, a comedian has no one to whom he can pass the buck. There he is, alone on the stage, expected to make his audience laugh. To think you can do that, you have to be a megalomaniac.

I admit I'm mad myself. Only a madman would consider embarking on such a career. And only a madman would attempt to explain it all.

I bet there are few people who imagine that Sir Harry Secombe is anything but an habitually hearty chap. Yet Harry confided to me that he very often got bouts of melancholy. It is not surprising when you think of all the energy that he is constantly using to make people laugh.

It's years since I met Frankie Howerd, but I remember working with him in the early *Variety Bandbox* broadcasts. He never relaxed. If you watched him rehearsing, you could not conceive that he might ever be the slightest bit jocular. His face was constantly scowling and the colour of it was almost grey. During refreshment breaks he never congregated with the other artistes.

I regarded Frankie as a mad genius. I was on a train with him once when I was already successful and he wasn't yet *quite* so successful. He spent the whole journey telling me how popular he was and about the house-records he'd broken. He told me exactly how I should conduct my career to be a success like him.

Whatever his secret was, it didn't give him time to look after his fingernails. I offered him a pre-lunch sherry and when he picked up the glass I noticed that all his nails were rough with jagged edges. It looked as if he'd been brick-laying for a couple of months.

Tony Hancock is one of the saddest examples I can give. When he was normal he was marvellous – very, very funny. But more often than not, he was drunk. He drank absolutely everything.

After he and his wife had been having lunch with me once, I discovered bottles of booze all over the place. Stuffed under sofas. Behind curtains. In the broom cupboard. The bottles were intact, not emptied. I assumed that Tony's wife had hidden them, hoping to slow down his drinking.

I knew Tony well. We had performed in films, on radio and on TV. He came to say goodbye to me before leaving for Australia. It really was goodbye because, while he was 'down under', he decided to give up the struggle and killed himself.

Sid Field was another who had an underlying sadness, almost a desperation, beneath the comic façade. He was a morose character, not improved by the fact that he was a heavy drinker. I never saw him drunk but, like Hancock, he would demolish whisky, crème de menthe, gin, barley-wine, in fact anything with alcohol in it that came along. True, drinking does appear to lift some people's inhibitions and help them to be funny, but it never helped me.

Sid was the person who most impressed me with his talent. He was so happy with his work and got a tremendous kick out of it. In *Piccadilly Hayride* we did a Shakespearian sketch together, in which he played King John and I played his cook, Simnel. I used to mince on with a blonde wig and green tights and say to Sid, 'Mawnin'! What do you want for breakfast?' Sometimes it took me five minutes to compose myself enough to say my line because Sid made me laugh so much. He never stopped ad-libbing. You had no idea what he would come out with. One night he looked at me and said, 'You iron!' This was cockney rhyming slang abbreviation for 'iron hoof'. In other words – he was calling me a poof!

When the show first opened there had been another spot where I used to heckle him from the stalls. But we had to give that up because I laughed too much.

What a marvellous performer Sid was. Night after night I stood and watched him play an old butler with sore feet, in a sketch called, 'Don't Shake It, Harvey'. The man's feet were so painful that he had to walk on the side of his boots — and the whole of the audience winced with Sid. A thing like sore feet, and he turned it into poetry. It was beautifully done.

Peter Sellers also had the ability to make me laugh, and vice versa. Why? A lot of it was to do with the fact that we both *knew* we tickled each other's funny-bones. No comedians I ever met disliked a bit of encouragement.

During the war when, for some reason, I was on one of those forts in the Thames estuary, I met Terry Scott and found that he was (unlike most comedians) an attentive and appreciative listener. Mind you, there weren't many other distractions on a fort in the middle of the Thames. He laughed so much, when I told him some cockney stories, that I feared he was going to fall overboard.

One of the stories he liked was about a fat woman on a bus who opened her shirt-front and started to get ready to feed her baby. The baby didn't want any and pushed the breast away. Sitting opposite was a prim, middle-aged gentleman in black coat, striped trousers and bowler hat. The cheery cockney woman said loudly to her baby, 'Come along, dear. Have your din-dins, otherwise I'll give it to the gentleman opposite.'

Variations on this theme, all rendered in my usual posh, gap-toothed style, reduced Terry Scott to tears.

While there were comedians who have had me holding my sides, others hardly made me smile. Old timer, Robb Wilton, was one of the former. A brilliant *raconteur*, he was intrigued to know *why* he had such an outstanding success every time he told me a tale. I could never define why. I just loved his stories (which were never blue) and the way he told them. They were original and I adored his approach to humour. He really knew how to make my funny-bone react.

I never much cared for Woody Allen's comedy, but this gag of his did appeal to me. In one of his movies he said when he was a child his family had been so poor they had had to live in a basement. And when his father wanted to commit suicide, he went to the basement window and threw himself up.

So many funny men are always on show, or think they ought to be, which is quite distressing. Kenneth Williams used to do his act all night, even when he was not working. He spent his whole time trying to get laughs. I much preferred him in a more subtle guise. He was pure joy in *Share My Lettuce*, with Maggie Smith, at the Lyric, Hammersmith (1957).

When I made, *It's a Mad, Mad, Mad, Mad World* (1963), which had a gigantic cast of funny-men, I was the only non-American, and I found it exhausting and embarrassing because they never relaxed. They were always 'on'. It was terrible. A typical example was the day we were having lunch in a tent at Long Beach when, instead of just sitting normally, getting on with their meal, everybody started to act up, trying to outdo everybody else. Milton Berle did an act. Dick Shawn did his. Sid Caesar and Phil Silvers joined in. And little Mickey Rooney, not to be left out, began methodically decorating his face with food. He hung slices of meat over his glasses. He stuffed carrots up his nostrils. And he rubbed salad cream into his hair. He just went on and on trying to steal the show. I caught Spencer Tracy watching my reaction and we raised eyebrows together.

On the first day of shooting that violently slapstick film, everybody behaved awfully badly and unprofessionally, trying their utmost to top one another in zany humour. That this could happen was quite extraordinary to me because I have never been able to see the point of trying to upstage another performer in a film; it just doesn't work. The things those comedians thought they could get away with was madness.

Stanley Kramer, who directed and produced, called for the 'rushes', watched what had been done and said, angrily, 'It's rubbish. I'm not going to print an inch of it. From now on you all do exactly what I tell you to do.'

When I first joined the company, Jonathan Winters was jealous of me and took against me, always referring to me as 'the rich Englishman'. It took a lot of pleading from producer Kramer to prevent him from reshaping my Bentley. Jonathan, who carried an axe as a prop, badly wanted to bash it through the bonnet of the car.

My Wildest Dream was a weekly TV panel-game, in 1956, in which I took part with three other comedians, Tommy Trinder, Alfred Marks and Eddie Gray (sometimes substituted by David Nixon.) Many critics slammed the show. The *Daily Telegraph* said: '*My Wildest Dream* seems to prove that four comedians, each extremely funny in his own right, cancel out one another when they appear together.'

The critics were right. It was a terrible show.

The first time I realized that people did actually listen to my broadcasts was in Combe Martin. One warm evening, I was strolling up the High Street, when suddenly – through the dusk – I heard a voice. It was an eerie voice and it took me a moment or two to place where it had come from. Then I saw an old lady leaning across the hedge. With an impish look, she asked me, very intimately, 'Where's your father?' 'He's in London,' I said. And then I realized what she meant, and laughed. She was referring to a story which I had broadcast a couple of weeks previously.

It was about a farmer's lad, too young to handle the hay-cart he was guiding. Suddenly, the two inside wheels dropped into a ditch and the hay-cart, with its enormous load of hay, thudded to the ground. A woman standing nearby said to the boy, 'You have made a mess, haven't you?' And the boy mumbled, 'I don't know what my father will say.'

The woman said, 'Never mind, son. Come into my house and have a nice cup of tea and a slice of cake.' So they went inside and the lad supped down his tea, bolted his cake and said, 'Very nice. But I don't know what my father will say.'

And the woman said, 'Never mind about your father.

Have another cup of tea and another slice of cake.' So the boy had some more, and when he had finished, he wiped the crumbs out of his eyes and said, 'I just don't know what my father will say.' And she asked, 'Where *is* your father?' 'Outside,' the boy replied. 'Underneath the hay.'

I had rather an arduous time when I did half a summer variety season, in Bournemouth, with 'Monsewer' Eddie Gray because Eddie was another person who never relaxed. Relentlessly, he was always playing jokes and he did the most extraordinary, sometimes quite preposterous, things. He seemed to have a genuine need for nonplussing people.

A stage-struck girl, who wanted an interview with him, was a perfect example of the lengths he would go to give himself a laugh. When she arrived at the stage-door and asked to see him he sent a message telling her to wait. After a minute or two, he phoned the stage-door keeper and told him to send the girl through.

'Do come in,' he called kindly, in answer to her timid knock on his dressing-room door. When she went in, 'Monsewer' Eddie was standing in his birthday suit. Confused, the girl exclaimed, 'I'm very sorry', and turned to leave. Eddie said, 'I thought you wanted to see me. Now what can I do for you, my dear?'

The poor girl did her best to behave as if nothing was amiss. 'I'd … er … I would like a job as a dancer. Can you help?' she said.

'I'll certainly see what I can do,' beamed Eddie. 'Come back and see me next week.'

'Thanks very much,' said the girl.

Then Eddie said, 'I wonder whether you would close your eyes for a minute. I want to put my trousers on.'

Don't try to work it out because most of Eddie Gray's humour was wild and quite impossible to explain.

Jimmy Edwardes played a merry wheeze on Al ('Right Monkey') Read, at St Anne's one summer, when we were all appearing in shows around there. Al was hooked on signing autographs; he really loved it! Jimmy knew that Al never turned away people who wanted his signature, no matter how late it might make him for an appointment. So he kept sending bits of paper into the St Anne's Hotel, where Al was drinking with some friends.

Al must have thought that six fan-clubs had arrived in coaches. If Jim hadn't eventually run out of paper, the signing session would have gone on indefinitely.

Jimmy once told me a story that pleased me very much. There was a church in Sussex that had a screen which needed repairing, so they got somebody to come down from London to do something about it. This chap was bashing away at the lovely old wood with a hammer when he gave his thumb a fourpenny one and cried out in pain. The language he used was not the slightest bit religious.

The vicar overheard this because he was on the other side of the screen. He was a bit of a ventriloquist and so he was able to throw his voice through the screen and make it seem as though the saint depicted on it was tearing the carpenter off a strip.

When he had finished, the vicar walked round the screen and said, 'Did you hear what the blessed saint said about reviling in the house of the Lord?'

The chap replied, 'Yes I did, and I don't understand it. I came in 'ere this mawnin', there was no place to 'ang me 'at, so I bunged a nail in his back-side and he didn't say a bleedin' word!'

I used to have a good rapport with Jimmy who was a frightful egoist, quite nauseatingly erudite. Anyone more erudite than I, I regarded as a real shower, but I liked Jim – a splendid, exuberant person! He stepped in for me and did an emergency edition of *How Do You View?* when I was taken ill with pleurisy in November 1951.

I hunted with Jim several times at his home near Edenbridge, Kent, Jim always resplendent in full hunting pink. Once, we were about to set off with the Old Surrey and Burstow Hunt when my horse, Rex, reared and tipped me off his back. Rex rolled on to me and my right arm was fractured in the confusion.

On another occasion I fell off my horse, Foxwing, and twisted my foot while riding in Rotten Row, just about the same time that Jimmy Edwardes and his horse were falling at the last jump of the Foxhounds Hunter Trials, in Sussex.

I sent a cable to Jimmy: 'Lucky you didn't fall on the horse.' He cabled back: 'Damnit, you've pinched the only decent gag.'

We became very close friends in Blackpool and I always thought I knew Jim and all the facets of his character very well; so I was surprised to read in the *Daily Express*, a few years ago, that he had come out of the closet and revealed that he was a poofter. I found it very difficult to accept because of the number of girl-friends he always had around him. I used to regard him, when we were both top of the tree and fit as a pair of fiddles, as one of the biggest rams I had ever come across. Women adored him.

I think he must have been AC/DC. During the war he risked his life, not to mention his moustache, flying backwards and forwards to Normandy picking up fighter-pilots stranded in mid-air, so to speak.

Peter Sellers and I made several films together. Soon after our first meeting, he strolled up to me at Elstree and complained, 'The trouble about my rôle is that they wanted an actor for it with a cockney accent. To me this is devastating because I've spent five years trying to *lose* my cockney twang.

He had lost it so successfully, by the time we made *The Naked Truth* (1957) that he confided to me, one day, 'I've come to the part of the film which is scaring me to death. I'm supposed to use my own accent. *And I haven't got one!*'

I never regarded Peter as competition. My ear was not good enough for some of the parts that he did. His great strength was in creating characters and he always gave himself a hard task when working on them. The difference between us was that he could use any accent he wanted. He could even invent accents which, to a certain extent, seemed to me to be a bit of a waste of time although it was highly effective in *I'm All Right Jack* (1959).

At home, though, he was not very exciting or amusing. Whenever I visited him and his family, he seemed just a typical suburban father. Perhaps that was because he lived in Barnet, which to me was another Finchley – dreadful!

I noticed quite a lot of uncertainty in Peter. People's zodiac-sign mattered to him and he relied on fortune-tellers to advise him on big decisions. In some things I felt he was rather underdeveloped. Tarts intrigued him and he was always keen to talk about them.

Peter was a notoriously difficult man, though I never had any trouble with him. Lionel Jeffries told me how Peter had misbehaved and caused a lot of fuss one day, on the set of *The Prisoner of Zenda*. That night, Peter phoned Lionel and asked, 'Was I really awful today?' When Lionel replied, 'Well ... yes,' envisaging that an apology would follow, Peter just gave a satisfied laugh, and rang off.

By mistake, Peter's price shot up quicker than it should have done in the normal course of events. In 1960, he was offered the lead in *The Millionairess* opposite Sophia Loren with the staggering, suggested fee of £85,000. Clairvoyant's advice was not necessary on this one. Peter accepted at once. Leonard Urry, the agent who made him the offer, was a good friend of mine and had not been dealing in films long. I asked him, 'What on earth made you give Peter so much?' And Leonard replied, 'I only offered what I thought was a fair price.' And I said, 'I suppose there's no reason why you shouldn't offer what you want. But it's hardly good business when you could easily have got him for £50,000.' I knew exactly what Peter had been earning up to then. After that, his price soared.

A feature of his character was that he always said exactly what he thought, something that very few actors could afford to do. Somehow Peter always got away with it, even when he was an unknown. He could also take a joke against himself, especially if it was unintentional. He told me this story concerning my sister Mary.

Mary, a person with very old-fashioned manners, was once in a hotel in Brighton when she saw Peter across the hall. He waved and walked over to her. 'Hello Mary.' 'Hello Peter, what are you doing here?'

'Well,' he said. 'I was going to Calais, but my new Rolls broke down so I've decided to spend my holiday in Brighton.'

'What a good idea,' said Mary, gently. 'You'll like this hotel. It's very quiet. And there are no Jews here.'

Peter leaned across the table and winked: 'Well Mary, there are now!'

Another incident involving my sister Mary, which illustrates different people's sense of humour, occurred on the day she and her late husband, John Ross, came to lunch with me and my second wife, Belinda. I will introduce Belinda properly in Chapter Six. Suffice it to say here that she was always so uninhibited, she would tell any story, anywhere, without hesitation or embarrassment.

During lunch, Belinda suddenly said, 'Tell them my favourite limerick.' 'You must be joking,' I said. And Mary and John chorused, 'Oh go on, Tom. Do tell us.'

'No,' I said, firmly. 'You wouldn't enjoy it at all.'

So Belinda said, 'If you don't, then I'll tell it.'

I jumped up ready to stop her by stuffing a napkin or a bread-roll down her throat; anything to prevent her telling this very crude limerick.

I didn't succeed because Belinda started to tell it on the run. It was a small kitchen where we were sitting, with two doors. She was able to run out of one door through the other, with me following fruitlessly behind her. As it was a two-way door system, I didn't stand a chance of catching her.

With a gay laugh, she began to sing: 'There was a young fellow named Berkin, Who was always jerkin' his gherkin'.'

I shouted: 'STOP IT! Please, that's enough.'

But as she ran, her voice gurgled on: 'His mother said,

"Berkin, stop jerkin' your gherkin. It was made for ferkin', not jerkin"'.'

To my surprise and relief, Mary collapsed with laughter. Never in my life have I heard her laugh so loudly. As for John, I thought we would have to send for the doctor.

After we made *The Heroes* (1974), on location in Egypt, Rod Steiger complained in Rome about my own 'strange sense of humour'. In the desert one day, we did his death scene and he certainly made a meal of it. As he hammed-up being hit by seven bullets consecutively, he mouthed a little prayer into the red-hot sky.

When I was certain that he had finished, I stepped from behind a lorry and walked towards him. I put my revolver back in its holster and said quietly to him, just as though we had finished a game of croquet, 'I say, old boy, are you all right?'

Apparently my manner quite put him off because when he went to Rome to add the dialogue, a few weeks later, he complained, 'I'm sure that Englishman was making fun of me, but I couldn't nail him down.'

Singer Tennessee Ernie (Ford) had a sense of humour I appreciated. He told me how he was once playing in a town in the middle of America and his wife was with him.

While Ernie went to be shaved, she popped out to do some shopping. A chap passed by, spotted him and exclaimed, 'Hey. You're Tennessee Ernie Ford, aren't you?' And Ernie said, 'Yuh, that's right!'

This chap thereupon rushed down the street shouting, 'Tennessee Ernie Ford is up there in that drug store.' Round the town he went, telling everybody he met. Eventually, he came across Mrs Tennessee Ernie Ford and said, 'Would you believe it if I told you that Tennessee Ernie Ford is in a store in this town?' 'Yes I would,' she said. 'I spent the night with him!'

Actor Jack Hawkins had a marvellous sense of fun. He told all his stories well, but one of them I liked so much that I asked him to repeat it every time we met and it never failed to make me chuckle. I'm not going to attempt to explain the joke – written down, it would be lost. It had to be told out loud ... by Jack!

Gilbert Harding too, was always good value, yet though we got on well together, I still considered him the rudest man I had ever met. I remember his rollicking a well-known London agent in such a way that everybody in the room could hear every word. Gilbert's monologue of complaints droned on for at least half an hour.

Joyce Grenfell always made me giggle. She was delightful. When we made *Blue Murder at St Trinian's* (1957) she used to have me in fits with her stories, mostly about her family.

There was the time her mother had urgently needed to contact an aunt, but hadn't her address. The only person who might know it was an uncle who lived in Buenos Aires.

So Joyce's mother sent a reply-paid international cable to him saying: 'Do you know Auntie Lilian's address?' Back came the reply: 'Yes!'

I thought both Beryl Reid and Dora Bryan were marvellous. And the late Hattie Jacques was very funny, besides being the nicest, kindest person one could wish to meet. When we were shooting *Make Mine Mink* (1960), I was chatting in the studio to Hattie when the wardrobe girl came up, excused herself and butted in to ask me if I had decided what I was going to wear for the next scene. I said, 'I think I'll wear the double-breasted chalk-stripe.' And Hattie gasped, 'WHAT?' I said, 'The double-breasted chalk-stripe.' 'Oh,' said Hattie, 'I thought you said the double-breasted jock-strap!'

Tessie O'Shea used to get big laughs in the North where she was very popular. Because of her size, she called herself Two Ton Tessie and after appearing with her at the Opera House, Blackpool, I discovered one of the reasons she was so fat. She used to consume masses of milk. She was always swigging milk. She literally got rid of gallons of the stuff, sometimes assisted by journalist Godfrey Winn, a great friend of hers.

Though it might seem strange, I always managed successfully to avoid appearing in variety films, by which I mean the 'Carry On' type of thing. I was never asked to take part in that particular series, but would have refused, anyway. I could never have been happy to appear in a film where I would be required to show my suspenders. One left that sort of thing to Norman Wisdom!

During the early part of this century, Harry Tate was the top comedian. He had a huge moustache, which he wiggled. His humour was existentialist, often cruel. The following true story is a good example.

Harry was once being driven down to Brighton by his son Ronnie Tate (known as Harry Tate Jr). They ran over a dog. Ronnie stopped the car, got out and started walking back towards a man who was carrying the dog which was obviously dead. 'I'm very sorry about this,' Ronnie said.

'It's all right your being sorry!' wailed the man.

'The dog ran under the car,' said Ronnie. 'There was nothing I could do.'

'All very well. You were motoring down the road at a hundred miles an hour.' (Ronnie's car would have fallen in half if it had been driven at over 18 mph.)

'I don't know what my wife will say,' moaned the man. 'This'll kill her.'

At this point, Harry who had just joined his son at the scene of the crime, remarked, '*Well then, don't let her eat any of it.*'

Sir George Robey was another old timer who had been an excellent entertainer. Sadly, by the time I met him, he was past it; his mind had gone. All he said to me was, 'I'm 84. I'm 84. I'm 84.'

Humourwise, Ted Ray was marvellous. He was one hundred per cent professional, even when doing his dirty stories. He never ad-libbed; always adhered strictly to the script. Charlie Drake I liked too; I thought he was excellent.

Max Miller's sense of humour is better revealed by this anecdote than by any personal opinion I might give. He

visited me in my dressing-room when I was doing variety in
Brighton. He sent the call-boy out for a couple of gin-and
tonics, and I thought, 'What style! What a compliment from
a great old-timer to an up-and-comer.' Max then proceeded
to try to sell me a second-hand Rolls. Unsuccessfully! What a
cheekie chappie!

Another cockney, Tommy Cooper, was funny both on and
off the stage. Just after the war we played in variety together,
and at Christmas 1950, we shared the cabaret spot at the
Royal Household party, Windsor Castle.

I had got Tommy his first break. Harry Meadows, the
owner of Churchill's Club, had asked me if I would play the
club again, but I turned it down. These shows didn't do me
any good. They made me stay up far too late and drink too
much.

I told Harry, 'I'll send you someone you will love, who will
do much better than I'd ever do, because he goes down well
with drunken audiences. His name is Tommy Cooper. Trust
me, you don't have to see him first, just book him. And I'll
be there on the first night.'

Harry did as I suggested. I went to Tommy's opening ...
and he was marvellous.

A number of comedians tried putting their humour on
record, when the LP business boomed in the Fifties. I made
two albums, 'Strictly T-T' and 'Terry-Thomas Discovers
America'; the first for Europe, the second for the USA.

I didn't realize, at the time, the importance of personally
promoting your record. A coast-to-coast itinerary was
worked out for me in America, but I was not convinced I
needed to do it. I didn't think it fair that I should have to pay
my own expenses for the trip. Had I been aware then how
much money was to be made from albums, I might have
given it a serious whirl!

Much to my annoyance, a colleague of mine decided to
perform some of my material straight from my albums. He
shouldn't have got away with it, but he did. I wrote him a
letter pointing out what an old member of the Savage Club

had said, when asked if he could return a fiver that had been lent to him. 'Certainly not,' replied the old stager. 'I haven't finished with it yet.'

If anyone would like to borrow any of the following, well-tried stories – unlike the fiver – they are finished with, as far as I am concerned.

A dog came up to me and I stepped sideways rather quickly. 'Don't worry,' its Irish owner said. 'He won't be after bitin' yuh.' 'Biting me?' I said. 'By the position of his leg, I thought he was after kicking me!'

*

I once saw a man who had a dog that could do the most fantastic tricks. The man used to get a piece of garibaldi biscuit (I suppose he could have done it with a digestive, too) and at a word of command – some filthy oath – the dog slid the biscuit down his tongue, threw it in the air and neatly caught it. I do wish you'd been there. It was fascinating.

I complimented the owner and he said, 'Yes, he is a clever dog. But he's a one-man dog. He wouldn't do it for anybody else.'

A chap wearing a sharp suit said, 'I'll bet you a fiver I can make him do what I tell him to.' 'You're on!' said the dog's owner. So the chap picked up the dog, put him on the fire and said, 'Now jump off.'

*

As I have plugged dogs, I think it only fair to give cats a mention. I was in a pub: the Old Cow and Crumpet. Lots of old cows, very little crumpet! And somebody was playing the piano. The man next to me said, 'Do you like the piano?' 'Yes I do,' I replied. 'Especially when somebody plays it.' (I was in ripping form.)

'I've got a cat that plays the piano,' he said. And I said, 'I've got a budgerigar that plays the flute.'

The man said, 'No, seriously, if you've got a few minutes, I'll take you back to my house and show you.'

I didn't think there was anything to lose, so off we went and a short while later arrived at a little semi-detached house and there was the cat – also semi-detached!

The man said, 'Ernie, give us a tune on the piano.'

And the cat, without any hesitation at all, jumped on the piano stool and started to play. He did very well although, he had a little trouble with the pedals. I said, 'This is marvellous. You ought to have him orchestrated.'

And, do you know? That cat was out of the door before you could say, 'Charlie loves Gertie.'

*

There was a chap who commanded the Kenya Regiment. This was the regiment that had all-white officers, with black privates. How contemporary can you get!

One day, he went to see an Indian grocer named Nuri and said, 'How about making a lot more money out of your business? I could arrange for two airplanes to fly over your stores, each trailing a banner behind it with some jolly slogans printed on the banners plugging your business.'

Nuri liked the idea and immediately gave the chap a cheque.

The day arrived for the airplanes to fly over the store as arranged. The first plane arrived, and the banner behind it read: 'Go and get stuffed'. A minute later, the second plane followed with this banner: 'Olives at Nuri's'.

*

A school teacher met the local vicar. And she said, 'You're the very man I wanted to meet. Do you think you could come to the school next week and talk to my girls about sex?' So he said, 'I should be delighted.'

That evening, he wrote in his diary: 'Speak to girls at St Margaret's about S...sailing.' He didn't want to put in sex, in case his wife saw it and mocked him.

A fortnight later, the vicar's wife met the schoolmistress who remarked, 'I can't thank your husband enough for coming to talk to my girls.' And the vicar's wife said, 'He was delighted. But I can't understand why he chose that subject.

He's only done it twice in his life. The first time it made him sick and the second time his hat blew off.'

*

A girl invited her chap for supper and said to him, 'You fancy yourself a bit of a know-all about wine. What do you think of this one?' He rolled the wine round his mouth, pondered professionally, and said, 'Well, it's not much. Burgundy perhaps? Very modest. I'd say £2. Am I right?' The girl said, 'You tell me. You ought to know. You gave it to me last Christmas.'

*

Sir Harold Macmillan was out with his gun on the Yorkshire Moors and he saw a girl running in front of him. He also observed that she was completely naked. Sir Harold noticed this because it was rather a cold day. And he said, 'What on earth are you doing?' The girl replied, 'I could ask you the same thing.' So he said, 'I'm looking for game.' And she said, 'Well, I'm game.' So he shot her.

5 Movies and Motives

My first rôle in a full-length feature, a modest rôle that was to launch me as an international screen actor, I initially turned down. I didn't think the part of the heavy-drinking major in *Private's Progress* (1956) was suitable for me. I'd have preferred to play a sergeant-major, so I said no. Had it not been for an agent named John Redway talking me into it, who knows what course my career might have taken? John was so certain I'd make a success of the part that he travelled from London to Nottingham to see me. He managed to persuade me that I had been mad to reject the offer. The Boulting Brothers had already recast, but John was able to get them to change their minds again.

The overhung major was only a small part, but lots of people thought he stole the picture. One of his lines: 'You're an absolute shower!' became a popular catchphrase.

Of course, after all those years as an 'extra', I was no stranger to filming techniques. Filming was similar to TV (I'd certainly done my share of that) and Alan Hackney's skilful dialogue made it an easy transition from the variety stage to the film-set.

I remember John Boulting, the producer, asking me to do an extra shot which he felt was missing. It was the part in the film where the major had taken an afternoon off to go to the local cinema. When the lights went up, the first thing the major noticed was that at least half his men had had the same idea. John said he needed a close-up of me registering shock, fury, indignation and anything else I could stuff in. He said, 'Remember all this when the camera is turning and you should get the right expression over.'

'Yes John,' I replied, 'I'll do that.' Actually, I didn't do anything. I just looked into the camera and kept my mind blank.

It is a trick I've often used since. In this way, the audience does the work. We shot it twice, for safety, then John said to me, pleased, 'Thank you, dear boy.' I was tickled pink when *Sight and Sound* nominated this scene as 'the best close-up of the year'.

Initially, I was not keen to accept my second part, either. I was offered 'the motor car salesman, with a beautiful car, who loses the girl to Alastair Sim' in *The Green Man* (1956). Very sure of myself, I told producer, Frank Launder, I didn't think the part was important enough for me. In the end I agreed to do it. I found George Cole one of the easiest people in the world to work with, and it was an experience to collaborate with Alistair Sim. You never knew exactly what he was going to do, and neither, I felt, did he. My personal opinion was that half the time he couldn't make up his mind how to play the part with the result that his performance was rather fey.

In *Brothers in Law* (1957), another Boulting Brothers' production, I played Alfie Green, a scruffy cockney spiv. To get the clothes right, I slept in them for a number of weeks and added to the effect by rubbing the seams of my suit with pumice stone.

My fourth film, *Blue Murder at St Trinian's* (1957) was quite uneventful for me, but a shaming experience for Lionel Jeffries. He was cast as the headmistress and this displeased him. In those days 'drag' was practically confined to *Charley's Aunt* and Lionel told me he felt very embarrassed and uncomfortable about the rôle. As far as I can remember, his wife, Eileen, had talked him into it.

Despite his discomfort, he was brilliantly funny dressed in a woman's Harris tweed costume. He didn't wear a wig, so his 'headmistress' was completely bald.

I was back on home ground for my scenes in *Lucky Jim* (1957) which were shot at Golders Green and Finchley. I played a pseudo intellectual with a beard and had to ride a small Vespa. Nobody thought of asking me whether I'd ever ridden one before, and seeing how handy I was on a horse, it didn't occur to me that I might have difficulty. The moment I got on the machine I realized I was in dead trouble. I hadn't a clue. The expression on my face must have been very funny. I saw the camera boy looking at me through his view-finder and howling with laughter. Eventually, I did get a sort of hang of the thing and I gave Hugh Griffith, who played my father, quite a ride. I finished up charging the camera, and the team scattered like skittles.

Hugh was annoyed that I had been cast as his son. At 45, he was ten months younger than I. 'I hope you've got a good make-up man,' he told me, loftily, and he had his own make-up man give him a very young face. Director Roy Boulting said to him, crossly, 'What on earth do you think you're playing at? Wash all that silly stuff off.'

While we were making *The Naked Truth* (1957), the first of three films I was to make with Italian producer/director Mario Zampi, I had a most unpleasant experience. In the plot, after I was supposed to have done some dastardly thing, Joan Sims and her screen mother, Peggy Mount, picked me up and threw me, fully clothed, into a lake. Shooting that scene, in a lake near Guildford, took some time. The awful thing about it was that there were snakes in the lake. They were buzzing round me the whole time I was in the water.

I was more than happy to get out and back to the pub. I'd always been scared of snakes since I was a kid and my brother's pet snakes escaped from their box. I was the one who had found them, unexpectedly, in the kitchen, all coiled up in a corner. Revolting! A true case of snakes and larders!

Peter Sellers made one of his 'protests' during shooting of *The Naked Truth*. He turned to Mario Zampi and shouted, 'The way you are making this film is ridiculous. You can't direct. I know much more about the camera than you do. I'll give you one more take and then I'm off.'

Mario didn't reply. He stood there, shocked.

The 'naked truth' was that Mario Zampi was never happy until he had got up to about the fiftieth retake of each scene. He was over-fastidious. For the actors, it was exhausting, frustrating and a pain in the arse to have to do the same scene over and over again when it was not really necessary. I always co-operated, but I suppose I was wrong. I should have made a stand, too, and not allowed Signor Zampi to get away with it.

At the end of that film, non-stop knitter Peggy Mount gave me a chunky blue sweater she had worked on during shooting, very well made with a hood that pulled up. I wore it when I used the open-topped motor car.

The Naked Truth was the second of three films I made with Dennis Price and I found him most likeable. He arrived every morning with a basket of beer slung over his shoulder – bottles of brown ale and stout; all pretty strong stuff. As the day went by he methodically got rid of it. All of it. Well, he was a very practical chap and he didn't want to carry any of it home.

I have already described *Tom Thumb* (1958) as my second favourite film. Peter Sellers and I played two thieves doing the dirty on two-inch-high Tom Thumb (marvellous performance from Russ Tamblyn). My part was perfect, but Peter's was bloody awful. He wasn't difficult about it, but he knew it. For the actors it was an extraordinary feeling to move in those giant sets amidst the huge tables and chairs built so as to enable Russ Tamblyn to appear minute. There was a crib 40 ft long and 30 ft high. And a teaspoon that measured 8 ft.

I have good cause to remember *Tom Thumb* because I had eighty-five days of an excruciatingly painful back and my rôle entailed running, riding a horse and fighting a duel with Sellers in which I leapt over a table just as I had seen Douglas Fairbanks Snr do in *The Mark of Zorro*. I had to swallow handfuls of codeine tablets so that I could move. Next time, *Tom Thumb* comes up on your TV screen, check! You can see I was in pain. Although it appears as if I'm doing a sinister, crablike walk, that walk wasn't put on. It was caused by lumbago.

I played the title rôle in *Carleton-Browne of the F.O.* (1958). Cadogan de Vere Carleton-Browne, only son of a senior official in the Foreign Office, was himself in charge of the Dept of Miscellaneous Territories. I described this man as being rubble from the nostrils up. My driver surprised me when he said, 'Enjoying this part, Mr T?' I said, 'Yes, very much.' 'Well,' he grinned, 'it's a bit of cake for you, isn't it?' 'What makes you say that?' I asked. And he replied, 'Well, it's *you*, isn't it?' My day was shattered.

The film was scheduled to be shown at the Moscow Film Festival in August 1959. But the Foreign Office 'banned' it the same day that it was selected.

High-ups at the Foreign Office strongly recommended the selection committee of the British Film Producers' Association and the Federation of British Film Makers to withdraw it. They feared the Russian audience might confuse high-bred idiot Carleton-Browne with normal British diplomats, a view endorsed by Sir (D'arcy) Patrick Reilly, the British Ambassador to the USSR. So the film selectors officially rejected it.

Peter Sellers was far from happy with his rôle in *Carleton-Browne*. He was much more at ease in the film we made together immediately after. For the first time he revealed what he could do so masterfully: create a character so well you forgot you were looking at Peter Sellers.

He played shop steward Kite in *I'm All Right Jack* (1959). This time Roy produced and his twin, John, directed.

I was a former War Intelligence Officer, Major Hitchcock, who had become a public relations man. There was a scene where I had to go to Mr Kite's house to try to get him to call off a strike. As far as I could tell, when we shot it, it was relatively simple for both of us and I could see nothing wrong with it. Peter, however, felt that his performance wasn't as good as it could have been. He really made a thing about it. I was just about to leave to start on another film when I was told we were going to have to do that shot all over again.

I had to get out my darning needle once more because I spent most of the scene mending one of Mr Kite's socks as his wife had left him. To reshoot, it must have cost the Boultings thousands.

It was a very big thing Peter had asked because the by-then-dismantled set of Kite's house had consisted of a mass of junk which had to be carefully matched up with previous shots. This retake was the one used in the film, but in all fairness to Peter I couldn't see any difference. His performance, to me, seemed identical to the first one.

When I made *Spanish Fly* (1975) on the Balearic island of Minorca, shooting was held up for two days because somebody had pinched my hat. The character I played wore a most unusual panama hat which had come from Bond Street, so unusual it couldn't be replaced locally. So when my hat disappeared and couldn't be found, there was pandemonium. The whole thing could have been reshot, minus hat, but it seemed easier to send to Bond Street for another hat. Production came to a halt and members of the company spent two sunny days, eating, drinking, swimming and sweating.

While making *Too Many Crooks* (1959) I was also appearing at the London Palladium. It was my third film that year. For my nervous system, I was doing too much. It was madness. I was getting up at seven, filming throughout the day, then performing twice-nightly with, on Saturday, a matinée performance as well. I took it for granted that I had to cram in as much work as I could. My meals were taken on the run.

One night I felt surprisingly wide-awake after the show and on the way home, I said to Bray, my chauffeur, 'I think I'll stop off for a couple of minutes.' Bray said, 'Now you're not supposed to do that.' 'I know I'm not,' I said. 'I'll just make it a flash.'

I went into Churchill's to have a few words with the owner, Harry Meadows – and drank a couple of buckets of champagne. Next morning, or should I say later that same morning, I arrived in my studio dressing-room feeling decidedly jaded. Hardly surprising!

I was just about to settle down for thirty winks when the call-boy arrived with a message from producer, Mario Zampi. Would I go to the set at once?

I floated after the call-boy. There was Mario in one of his noisy, Italian moods. 'Terry darling,' he said. 'I don't like this scene. What do you think?' 'Well,' I said, 'it won't win any Oscars.' So Mario said, 'It will take us a half-hour to light it, so would you just rewrite it?'

Somehow or other, despite my thick head, I managed to do something with the script and we moved on to a shot in which Peter Sellers played the part of an old man who was wearing a false moustache. The moustache had to fall off and there wasn't a line to cover my facial reaction. Peter said to Mario, 'What do you want me to say?' And Mario asked me, 'Terry, what should he say?' Jokingly I said, 'Why not "I've got a touch of the creeping alopecias"?' Peter giggled and agreed, 'That'll do.'

That was one thing I always noticed about Peter: ad-libbing was never his strong point. Still, it didn't seem to do him much harm, did it?

All comedians are expected to come up with special material. I have contributed hundreds of funny lines to the scripts of my films. Yet apart from personal satisfaction, there were no 'perks' attached. I was never paid extra or given any credit.

Although *School for Scoundrels* (1960) was based on Stephen Potter's books on one-upmanship, it was not all

Potter. I, too, contributed quite a lot of material and during shooting I became very friendly with Potter; a relaxed man, full of charm.

One suggestion of mine, when shooting a scene with Edward Everett Horton in *The Perils of Pauline* (1967) was unceremoniously rejected by the joint producers, a husband-and-wife team. I still maintain that it was a harmless bit of business and not as vulgar or offensive as they claimed. In the film, Edward Everett Horton and I were supposed to be billionaires. When a waiter brought us drinks, Edward had to say, 'I'm the richest man in the world', to which I replied, 'I'll drink to that – Cheers!' But the scene kept failing. A line was missing. I had an idea which I explained to Edward. Then I told the producers, 'When we do the scene next time, we will change a line and put in another. Take my word, it's going to get a very big laugh.'

The waiter brought our drinks. 'Cheers!' we said, and downed our glasses. 'Uuuuurgh, what *is* this?' I asked Edward. And he replied, 'Mother's milk.' I then made a face of disgust, promptly spat it out and said, 'No wonder babies cry.'

Everyone in the studio laughed except the two producers. 'You can cut that out,' they both said, tight-lipped. I could have kicked them but I didn't bother to discuss it further. I realized that this wasn't their sort of humour; they clearly both looked upon motherhood as sacred.

Yet another of my suggestions that didn't make it was a joke I wrote for the bedroom scene between Ann-Margret and me in *The Last Remake of Beau Geste* (1976). We were in bed together. I wanted Ann-Margret to ask me, 'Why are you wearing that overcoat?' And I would have replied, 'A man in my position can't be too careful.'

But Marty Feldman, who was enjoying himself hugely both directing and playing a big part, decided not to use it. I don't know why, it wasn't blue. Yet he allowed the line where, as Ann-Margret's exhausted victim, I told her, 'You have made a happy man old.' That didn't make much sense either, but it *was* a wild comedy.

I confess I found it embarrassing doing that scene cuddled up in bed with the Swedish-born actress. Ever since my early days in amateur dramatics I had been bothered by erections whenever I was acting with a girl. (This obviously didn't apply if she had a heavy moustache.) Ann-Margret was stunning, absolutely gorgeous; so acting with her at such close proximity was understandably hard-on me, so to speak.

The delightful Athene Seyler was a great leg-puller and it was stimulating to work with her in *Make Mine Mink* (1960), screen adaptation of the stage comedy *Breath of Spring*. Athene played the part she had created on stage, an aristocrat who engaged a gang of people to go round pinching furs in order to sell them to raise money for charity. An ad-lib of Athene's in one of my scenes with her became an in-joke on the set. I had to say, 'Why do you think this robbery should take place on a Wednesday?' She replied, 'Because it's the maid's day off.'

Then she quickly rectified the 'off' to 'awf' as no upper-class person would pronounce the word any other way than with the long vowel-sound. It was put into the film and for days afterwards the crew kept deliberately correcting themselves whenever the word 'off' came up in conversation.

Dumpy little Irene Handl was also in *Make Mine Mink*. She was a quaint person, with a quaint appearance to match. Even her dogs were quaint. They were chihuahuas; she always had more than one with her. Fortunately, the dogs were shut in her dressing-room while she was on the set. I was perpetually afraid that Irene was going to step on a pooch and go down, because even at 55, her age when we did *Private's Progress* (the first of our three films together) Irene was already tottery on her legs, and she got worse.

I got my first bad notices since I had started in films with MGM's *A Matter of Who* (1961). This was a semi-documentary with suspense and comedy thrown in. I played my first (fairly) serious role, a man connected with the World Health Organization, whose job it was to trace germs. There had been an outbreak of smallpox and the most athletic germ that was the cause was hopping about all over the Austrian Alps. I eventually traced it to Orwald.

The writer and joint-producer, Milton Holmes, was a great T-T fan and had been convinced that T-T was an actor of such integrity he would play the role exactly as it was written. He had made a mistake. The Press, led by writer, Tom Wiseman, accused me of making fun of smallpox victims. I felt bruised and indignant, and when we met at the Village Club, Chelsea, I lost no opportunity of telling Wiseman clearly and precisely what I thought of him.

It had been a thrilling experience making that film because I had had to do such hair-raising stunts. In one of them I drove underneath a moving lorry, in an open-topped Austin 7, and came out the other side.

The secret of the stunt was that both the car and the lorry should rigidly keep to a constant, previously worked-out speed. Neither driver could accelerate or slow down. First, I walked over the distance of road we would use for the shot, looking for potholes.

Once I'd got the feeling for it, it did not seem highly dangerous. But it could have been. Looking back, it was strange that Milton Holmes allowed me to do it. I didn't have to do stunt-work, and got no extra money for it. Sometimes, I have refused to do things because I knew they were impossible for me. But more often than not, I was intrigued; I wanted to do it to see how it felt.

There was another scene where I had to speed down Queensgate, turn left into a *cul de sac*, cut through a gap in the traffic and come out into Queensgate again. There were only six inches to spare as I whizzed through the gap, but I did it first time. That was very thrilling.

The most unpleasant stunt was going 10,000 feet up an Austrian alp in a ski-lift that had no floor. The director had had it removed because he wanted to shoot from below. I had to stand legs apart resting my feet on ledges on either side of the contraption. Hair-raising to say the least.

Walter Shenson, Milton Holmes's fellow-producer, once invited me to a party in his flat where The Beatles turned up. (Walter produced their films *A Hard Day's Night* and *Help*). It was one of those stand-up parties where it was easy to circulate for there was just a drinks table, a couple of waiters and no chairs. The Beatles, who were very new to London, stuck together and kept saying to one another, over and over again, 'What a foony parteh. No chairs!' The more they repeated it, the 'foonier' it became to the rest of us. In the end, John, Paul, Ringo and George were laughing as much as anyone.

Frank Tashlin, director of my first Hollywood movie, *Bachelor Flat* (1961) was another person who thought that T-T was wonderful, which gave a big boost to my morale while making my début in Tinsel Town. I felt a bit insecure. New projects – like facing Hollywood for the first time – always gave me first-night nerves.

Tashlin had been a number-one director (*The Paleface* with Bob Hope and Jane Russell; *The Girl Can't Help It* with Jayne Mansfield) but by the time we met he had fallen by the wayside a bit. Like so many in Hollywood, he was a heavy drinker. He died in 1972.

In an early scene, I had to climb a 30-ft ladder, which was leaning against the side of a burning house, and hand Tuesday Weld, the teenage star of the film, a cup of tea.

When I came down the ladder, I was sweating as though I'd been under a shower. For that sequence I was all dolled up as a soldier in the Confederate Army and my uniform was wet through.

Frank Tashlin asked me, 'What's the matter, Terry? You look as though you have been pissed on by an elephant.'

I said, 'I'm allergic to heights.'

'Why didn't you tell me before?'

'I like to do my own stunts.'

'That's all very well,' said Frank, 'but there's no need to

bust a gut.'

What I remember most about *Bachelor Flat* was the extraordinary behaviour of Tuesday Weld. She earned herself the distinction of being the most frightening person I had ever come across – a title she still holds.

She was an unknown, but behaved like royalty. I thought she lived the most dangerous life; quite shocking! She used to drive a car as long as the *Queen Mary* and park it anywhere, whether there was a vacant space or not. She would drive up on the pavement, unconcerned whether or not she was blocking someone's access. She would just leave the car, often with the engine running, then gaily walk away.

Yet Tuesday was a good performer. When acting, she was not at all difficult as were so many other Hollywood stars. It was just off-stage that Tuesday did not conform. Mind you, she was only seventeen at the time. Mere teenage exuberance and *joie de vivre* were probably the reason for everything. I imagine she calmed down as she got older, otherwise however did she became Mrs Dudley Moore after Dudley's divorce from the dazzling Suzy Kendall?

Richard Beymer, who was her co-star, was the exact opposite of Tuesday: very quiet-mannered, modest and soft-spoken. He was clearly a bit embarrassed by me because although he was billed as the star, he hadn't as much experience of comedy work. He made a very big point of the fact to the Management.

'Terry-Thomas's name should go first. He knows what he's doing. I'll willingly take second billing,' he said.

So my name took top billing in my Hollywood film début. Come to think of it, I didn't ask for any more money. I was a Charlie!

I flew to Gibraltar to make *Operation Snatch* (1961), a title that caused a few headaches when the film was shown in America! I played the lieutenant in charge of the Rock's Barbary apes and I recall a very funny piece of business with Lionel Jeffries when we were inside the apes' cage. Lionel whispered to me, 'Go and get a sack, or something, to put the ape in.' I found a sack, pushed it into the cage, and slammed the door shut. Lionel immediately panicked and shouted, 'Get me out of here, you gap-toothed git.' An amusing line considering it was addressed by a lance-corporal to an officer.

I then had an hysterical seizure which was started off by a junior assistant whom I saw laughing himself sick, hidden behind a packing case. I had told this fellow to keep out of my way because, earlier, he had created an enormous amount of trouble by not being able to control his mirth. I knew that if I saw anyone doubled up I would be crippled myself. And that's how it turned out. The assistant was banished and we completed the scene.

More diversion was caused when an ape bit right through the ear of one of the actors. That was not in the script. Richard Villiers (who was related to the royal family) clutched his bleeding ear and let flow the roughest line of language that I'd heard since I had left Smithfield.

There was a starry cast in MGM's *The Wonderful World of the Brothers Grimm* (1962) but I didn't meet many of them because we did not share scenes. It was a situation that often happened. Somebody said to me the other day, 'You and Claire Bloom were both in *Brothers Grimm*, weren't you? What's she like?' And I answered, quite innocently, 'Good Lord, was she in it too? I didn't know!' And I hadn't known.

My memory of my part as a cowardly knight in the 'Singing Bone' part of the film was that I had to hit my head hard against the top of a cave, a shot which took a long time setting up – much to my stand-in's discomfort.

I fervently wished that I'd used a stand-in and not done my own stunt in *Kill or Cure* (1962), a murder farce set in a nature clinic. I had to be strapped upside down to a spinning steel pillar, as part of the treatment I was supposed to be having in the clinic. I was very silly to have agreed to do it myself because while it might have looked fascinating on the screen, it hurt like blazes. There were not many retakes. I just couldn't stand it.

My rôle in *It's a Mad Mad Mad Mad World* (1963) was another that I initially turned down and then changed my mind about. When I was first approached, in Hollywood, I said, 'No, I don't like the script.' I then left for London but by the time I arrived I was having second thoughts.

From the airport I telephoned producer Stanley Kramer and said I'd like to do it after all. I grabbed some sandwiches and popped back on a plane to be fitted for the part.

With so many big names on set at the same time, one had to be very, very tough to hold one's own and not take it all too seriously. Off the set I spent a great deal of time with Ethel Merman. There was absolutely nothing negative about Ethel. She was always telling you what to do, and you did it! I did, anyway. She advised me how to dress. She took me shopping. Told me exactly what to buy. She literally hit me between the shoulder blades and pushed me around all over the place. She was so colourful and I was so amused by her that I let her get away with it. We lived extravagantly in every sense of the word.

After a week or two, Stanley Kramer asked me how I was enjoying myself and I said, 'All right. But it's pretty tough going.' 'Why?' he asked. 'Well, not only am I the only non-American in this huge cast,' I said, 'but also the only non-Jew.' (But now I come to think about it, I'm not certain about Spencer Tracy, though he was smart enough to be one.)

Stanley said nothing, just smiled his twisted smile.

We were shooting a fight scene once when his amusement proved to be rather costly. I had to climb out of an upturned car, scramble to the top of a bridge and jump off the side to get away from Dick Shawn who was pursuing me. When he caught me, Dick started to twist my head off, with the words, 'Are you English?' 'Why?' I asked. 'Don't you like the English?'

And it was at this point that Stanley Kramer burst into his ill-timed laugh, completely ruining the shot. It was the eighteenth take and the temperature was 115 in the shade.

Everything had to be done yet again, so Stanley's uncontrolled mirth was expensive. But as the film cost over two million dollars to make, I don't expect anybody noticed.

Dame Margaret Rutherford came up to me in a field at Pinewood while I was wearing a haystack. For my part in *The Mouse on the Moon* (1963) this had been fitted to my shoulders and I'm sure the effect of seeing a haystack nipping purposefully across a field towards the refreshment room was rather odd.

Dame Margaret poked her head into the stack and said, 'I would like your advice.' 'Well, make hay while the sun shines. I'll do what I can. What's the trouble?' I said.

And she said, 'I have just been offered a contract to make six films for this production company. What would you advise me to do?' She obviously had no idea what the films were, so I said, 'I would tell them to stuff it.'

'It sounds delightful, but why?' she said.

So I pointed out, 'What six films? They're probably not written yet and it's a hell of a gamble. You should wait until they've got the scripts and then you can judge whether they're good enough for you to play in them or not.'

I added, 'In any case, why would a person like you want to tie yourself up for six films?'

And she said, 'Well, one does like security, doesn't one?'

These words struck me as being rather quaint because she was highly popular and never out of work.

She had an agreement that her husband, Stringer Davis, should play in every film she was in. She had a Morris Minor motor car. And her idea of a banquet was a sausage roll and a sprig of parsley. I assumed that she must be saving up to be the richest actress in the cemetery. (She died, nine years later, aged eighty. I've never found out how much she left.)

While making *How To Murder Your Wife* (1964), Richard Quine, the director, had an annoying habit of giving me an early call and then not using me until midday. One day I went to him and said, 'I wish you would try to avoid calling me on the set early in the morning and then not using me for hours. It really is most upsetting.'

He got very annoyed and accused me of all sorts of nonsen-ses, none of which were true. So I said, 'I'm going back to the hotel, and if you need me, just apologize and I'll rejoin you.'

A couple of hours later, Jack Lemmon phoned me and said, 'Richard is most distressed and very sorry that he was so rude and would you please come on to the set?'

So I said, 'Sorry, Jack. The apology has got to come from Richard.'

The director did phone, about ten minutes later, and reluctantly apologized. I felt just as badly as he did about the incident, but it's no good letting people get away with bad behaviour. So I quickly had a think and came up with an idea how I could make my return as pleasant as possible.

I went into the hotel doctor's surgery and asked if I could have a bit of sticking plaster and dressing liberally splattered with blood, which I stuck to my face.

It looked as though I had just had a brick or something thrown at me. Had this been genuine, we should have been in serious trouble because obviously I wouldn't have been able to go in front of the camera with a badly wounded face and filming would have been held up.

When we arrived at the place where they were shooting, I jumped out of the car, went up to Quine and called, 'Richard!'

He turned round, took in the blood and bandages and for one hundredth of a second fell for it. We all had a bit of a cackle and continued with the day's work.

How To Murder Your Wife, for which I earned my highest fee to date – £100,000 – turned out to be my favourite film. I liked it because I felt that I did a very good job. Leading lady, Virna Lisi, straight from Italy, was unusually beautiful and voluptuous. It was her first American film and she could hardly speak a word of English when she started. But she refused to be dubbed. She dedicated herself to studying English grammar and by the time the film was made she was able to deliver her lines most attractively.

Jack Davies, the writer and producer, asked me to meet him at Lord's cricket ground one day. He was going to watch cricket and knew that I lived near by. He took me up in the bleachers where we were almost alone. Nevertheless, he lowered his voice to a whisper. In the film business, one could never be too careful. 'I've written the best part you've ever had,' he told me. 'Good show,' I said, in a hushed voice.

He was right, because the film was *Those Magnificent Men in Their Flying Machines* (1965).

I did a stunt in the film that gave me nausea. I did a shot where I was running along the top of a train which was hurtling towards a tunnel. The carriages were trembling under me as I wobbled along, jumping from wagon to wagon. It was hair-raising.

Magnificent Men was so successful that there was a follow-up, *Monte Carlo or Bust* (1968). The magic of the cinema made it look as if we were all flying solo in our small planes, but of course, we weren't. All done by trick photography and stand-ins who were professional pilots. We actors did not actually take off. When we felt our planes were about to 'float', we eased the stick forward ... and stayed on the ground.

Once, I was filmed standing up in a glider, 1,000 ft above the Sutton Bank Flying Club, at Kilburn in Yorkshire. I had to wave my hands and look excited. Not too difficult to look excited in that situation. The shot took just a few seconds to do, and though I wasn't scared, it seemed longer. I had needed a lot of persuading before agreeing to do it. But I couldn't have been tipped out because there were various things I could have clung to, had the glider tilted. (That's how they convinced me, anyway!)

The wind soared through the wires, or the other way round, and down below it was all very beautiful. The effect was like tap dancing on the cross of St Paul's Cathedral – although I haven't done that (well, not recently.)

Few film companies could afford to take risks with their performers' lives. The insurance cover would not allow it. I remember appearing in a French production when a stuntman was killed. He had taken the day off, without permission, to work on another film in which he had to crash a car. He died in the crash.

Denholm Elliott refused to climb a tree when we made *You Must Be Joking* (1965). I didn't blame him. It was a very difficult tree to get up and I wouldn't have done it myself.

I've seen people do things they must have known would injure them. Once, I was supposed to jump from a high wall. I wouldn't attempt it because I knew I wouldn't get away with it. I felt there was not sufficient room to manoeuvre myself into the right position to land. I would never attempt anything I wasn't sure of. A stunt-man stood-in for me – and broke his leg. See, there *hadn't* been enough room. Silly berk!

On another production, eight people were injured, some very badly, when two trains collided in San Fernando Valley. It was especially terrible for the script-girl who had practically all her bones broken.

I had to be filmed on one train and Milton Berle on another, both travelling in the same direction. Same scene shot from different angles.

Fate decided to let them shoot Milton Berle's scene first, otherwise I would have been on my train when it crashed. As it was, I stayed behind in the hotel that day, while Milton went off to work. He was not involved in the collision, but witnessed the whole thing. Instead of one train forking off to the right, at the junction, the points failed and the trains ploughed into each other. The company decided to take the insurance money. We were paid off, in full, and the film was never completed.

Another one I appeared in has never been shown anywhere – as far as I know! *Arthur Arthur* (1970), in which Shelley Winters and Donald Pleasence also took part, seemed to be full of possibilities. Texas oil man, Ted Weiner, who put up nearly £500,000 to finance the movie told the *Daily Express* in May, 1969: 'I liked the script and put up all the money. I don't necessarily want to make anything from it. But I don't want to lose, either.'

Portentous words. When I did my scenes by the river at Richmond, and in the studio in Camden Town, I couldn't help noticing that the director seemed to be under a great deal of stress and was frequently seen to be drinking. Gradually, filming slowed and eventually came to a grinding halt. I have a shrewd suspicion that the director drank so much champagne he didn't know what the film was about any more.

My first scene had been with Donald Pleasence who had been funnier than I had ever seen him before. We were in a pub in St John's Wood and a dog – a rottweiler – was supposed to bound up to me in a friendly way. The handler gave the wrong command, however, and suddenly the dog had my arm gripped firmly in its mouth.

What an awful experience to feel your arm being crunched! A nasty moment indeed, until the handler called the dog off. Donald was tickled pink. So was my arm!

Luck was with me when I made *The Heroes* (1974), an international co-production, produced by Duccio Tessari. In one scene, as a British Intelligence Officer, I had to jump up from a trench and run towards a gun emplacement, to storm it. The Italian in charge of the gun got so caught up in the action that he fired when I was just a few yards away from it. This was a misunderstanding, to say the least, as I had been expecting nothing. Fortunately I escaped unhurt but because of that man's incompetence, I might have been badly injured.

The Heroes was made in Egypt and, like so many visitors to that country, Rod Taylor had tummy problems. He knew from past experience that the only effective cure for this constipation was green peppers, but they were not easy to find. He sent his man to search greengrocers' shops and market stalls all over the city, but it was a nigh impossible task. At last, a small supply of the elusive vegetable was obtained and then guarded like a gold cache in the hotel kitchen. It was nice to see that strained expression disappear from Rod's face. 'Remember green peppers,' he told my wife, with a happy grin. 'They work like a charm every time.'

Rod Steiger was also in the film. I discovered that beneath that burly exterior, he had a big, soft centre. His affectionate side took the form of 'nannying'.

We used the same hotel and he was always behind me, fussing around me and trying to organize me. I politely requested him not to 'nanny' me, but it did no good. So I was quite relieved when he finished his part and left the company. It was nice to be without him. 'Now,' I said, 'We can have a quiet lunch for a change.'

But Rod Steiger was still there in spirit. It was my birthday and suddenly, an extravagantly decorated cake was brought to the table in all its dubious glory. There was a decoration on it picked out in coloured icing which was supposed to represent me showing my monocle and the gap in my teeth. It was quite the most vomit-producing caricature I had ever seen.

So horrendous was this cake there was nothing else to do but eat it at the speed of light. And it was delicious. Rod had organized the cake before he left. Inscribed across the top of it, in startling crimson writing was 'Happy Birthday Dear Terry. "Nanny".'

Throughout my film career, I have been billed as a guest star. Sometimes, the parts have been substantial and sometimes mere cameos. In many of the foreign productions, never seen in Britain, my work was done so quickly, I never even knew the title of the films or met the stars. Many's the time I have finished one picture on a Saturday and been flying somewhere on the Sunday to start shooting on the Monday. I loved to work and I loved to work fast. Rome one week, Paris the next, Brazil the week after. It was madness.

In *Who's Who*, forty of my films are listed, but if the foreign productions were to be included (those in which my part was completed in a couple of days) that list would be over 150.

A Press-man at 20th Century-Fox asked me why I, being a big star on both sides of the Atlantic, would accept such small parts in films. The answer was simple: 'Because,' I told him, 'I haven't the time to play big roles.'

In July 1967, the *Sunday Mirror* reported that since September of the previous year, I had taken part in ten films. By the time twelve months were up, I would add three films to the total. They quoted me as saying: 'I know it sounds utter madness. But the truth is that every rôle is such a gem that I'd hate myself for ever if I turned them down — especially if, for instance, Peter Sellers took them.'

Some agents were surprised when I turned down a supporting role in the highly successful TV series, *Two's Company*, with Elaine Stritch and Donald Sinden. One man said he was amazed that I felt I could afford to reject the series, seeing as the cast was so strong and the script so well written. To me, the only thing wrong about it was the fee. Quite unsatisfactory. Ridiculous, in fact, compared to what I was earning in films. These deals had to be equitable. I had almost fainted when I heard how little they wanted to pay me. My price at the time was £5,000 a day.

An outrageous incident in *Strange Bedfellows* (1966) is often in my mind. Rock Hudson was supposed to carry Gina Lollobrigida upstairs, and he couldn't do it. At 6 ft 4 in, with a name like Rock and a massive, muscular frame to match, he couldn't hold her for more than one-and-a-half seconds. I could only assume that La Lollo had her bra stuffed full of sand, or something.

The scene was successfully mocked-up by placing Gina on two planks supported at each end by a studio technician. All four unseen technicians and Rock, with Gina perched on the planks, moved in perfect synchronization up the stairs to make it look as if Rock was holding Gina. I rather hoped that something would go wrong. The resulting mess would have been hilarious.

Wilfrid Hyde White and I appeared in a couple of films together. He was famous in the business for the thick overcoat he always wore wherever he was, whatever the weather. While making *Our Man in Marrakesh* (1966) in which I played a desert chieftain with a Noël Coward accent, Wilfrid and I were sitting by the pool of our Moroccan hotel with other members of the team. Then the stunt-man came along and posed nonchalantly on the diving-board in a very abbreviated pair of shorts. It was a beautiful spring morning and Wilfrid, as usual, had his overcoat wrapped around him.

He glanced at the bulging stunt-man, did a double-take, then called lightly to somebody on the other side of the pool, 'What do you think he's got in there, d'you suppose? A bunch of asparagus?'

In Brazil I had snake trouble again when I made *Kiss the Girls and Make Them Die* (1966), a James Bond sex-comedy spoof, produced by Dino di Laurentis. Rio was marvellous, but there were just a few too many snakes for my liking. I was doing a scene when the cameraman made a movement with his hand and arm like a snake rearing to strike while giving a few practice jabs in my directions. I disappeared very quickly.

The assistant director said, 'Don't worry, Terry, that snake doesn't bite.' I said, 'What's he making that menacing movement for, then?' I didn't hang around to find out. I got into the Rolls and waited until they had caught the snake. This they did with their hands and then tied it by the jaws to the tubular hinges of the car boot. Uggggh!

It was cold up in the mountains above Dublin where we were on location for *Jules Verne's Rocket to the Moon* (1967). So cold that, to keep warm, Lionel Jeffries steadily knocked back whisky and/or brandy all day, in true Irish style. When the time came for us to go down the mountain at the end of the day's filming, Lionel couldn't move. Two members of the team put him in a hammock and carried him down between them. I can see Lionel now, draped in that hammock with the most absurdly vacuous grin on his face.

Lionel was an extraordinary man who shamelessly overacted and actually boasted about it. He was a perfect example of an eccentric actor who always played his cards in his own way and he had a reputation with directors and actors alike as a man to be watched.

I knew from experience because I worked with him several times. When we made *You Must Be Joking* (1965) Lionel had outrageously overplayed and every minute I waited for the director, Michael Winner, to say, 'Come off it, Lionel. I only want one performance. I'm certainly not paying you for two.'

But – as usual – Lionel got away with it.

On second thoughts, perhaps I wasn't surprised that Michael Winner didn't object, because, with all his talent, Michael never – in my opinion – directed anybody.

He was another delightful eccentric and a terrific show-off with whom I had many laughs. He often wore black coat, striped trousers and a white shirt with no collar; to my eye, pretty Bohemian at that time.

I'd known Michael since he was a boy when he used to be brought to my dressing-room, in West End theatres, by his father. He was charming, but thoroughly spoilt, always given anything and everything he wanted. As a child he had always got his own way, and still did as an adult.

Gene Kelly directed *A Guide for the Married Man* (1967) and to my disappointment, I found him a very prudish director, not as imaginative or experimental as I would have liked. He seemed to do everything he could to flatten the script. I had to go to the producer once, to keep a line in. It was the scene where Jayne Mansfield had left her brassière in my bedroom and she said to me, 'Don't bother about it. Your wife will find it and think that it's one of hers.' To which I was scheduled to reply, 'Look, if my wife could mistake one of your bras for one of hers, you wouldn't have been here in the first place.'

It was my reply that Gene wanted to cut. He would not explain his objection to the line, but I gathered he thought it was vulgar. The producer upheld my appeal and the line was left in.

Everything about Jayne Mansfield was exaggerated, not just her superstructure. When I was invited to call on her, it was clear that nobody ever saw red in her house. Wherever you looked you saw pink. Even in the bathroom there were pink fur rugs. Barbara Cartland would most definitely have approved.

There were pink chair-covers, pink cushions, pink pictures in pink frames, pink lampshades and a smashing pink bed in a pink room. Jayne was wearing a pink skirt with a pink top and pink slippers. 'Pink's my favourite colour,' she told me. 'No!' I said, trying to sound surprised.

Next day, however, she arrived in the studio with not an inch of pink to be seen. She had on a man's dark suit, black trilby hat and a pair of men's moccasins. Considering she was a sex symbol I found her rather intelligent to talk to and felt quite shattered when I read about the gruesome car accident that killed her, not long after we made that film together.

Don't Look now ... We're Being Shot At (1967) was a French production which had international distribution. The original title was *La Grande Vadrouille* and two of France's top comedians, Bourvil and Louis de Funes, shared the billing with me. We filmed while travelling through the centre of France, and ate jolly well on the way. The most notable thing that comes to mind is that the film was so successful at the box office that it made producer, Robert Dorfmann, a millionaire. The critics at home did not rave about it, though they were nice to me.

'Terry-Thomas works hard. He always works hard,' said the *Daily Telegraph*. 'But he vanishes from the film for long periods of time, presumably in search of a farce less demonstrably hybrid.'

In *Where Were You When the Lights Went Out?* (1968) I came up against the situation of having a leading lady, Doris Day, whose husband, Marty Melcher, was joint producer. So how WAS one to react when the producer's wife started to hand out free acting lessons?

Doris was clearly a woman who took herself very seriously indeed. 'Now Terry,' she'd say briskly, 'in this next scene, when we're standing over there, I suggest that you ...'

She would then proceed, in detail, to tell me exactly how she thought I should perform.

I had experienced this sort of thing when I appeared with Ethel Merman (*It's a Mad Mad Mad Mad World*), with Gina Lollobrigida (*Strange Bedfellows*) and with Debbie Reynolds (*How Sweet It Is* – 1968). They had all 'taught' me to act. Of course, I've always been open to suggestions. I mean in life you never finish learning. But these intense actresses were not just suggesting, they were *telling* me what to do. With the exception of Ethel Merman, they were younger than I, so I figured that as they were less experienced, it was unlikely that they could know better than I how to tackle my rôle. Even in the case of old-timer Ethel, I considered it would be impossible for her to know how a character like the one I was portraying would behave.

My reaction had been to listen to them politely, then do it my own way, as if the conversation had never taken place. I did the same with Doris Day.

In the middle of a shot, Doris would suddenly be struck by verbal inspiration. Disconcertingly, she would add to her lines. She would ramble on and on while the cameras turned until I began to wonder, 'Where *is* all this dialogue in *my* script.'

When I managed to dart an interrogating, raised-eyebrowed look at the director, Hy Averback, he shrugged apologetically, and with his hand high made a scissor movement behind Doris's head. He meant he was indulging his producer's wife, but would cut out her surplus material later – including a large number of pauses, long, long pauses.

Doris rode a bicycle a great deal and wore the oddest clothes I'd ever seen. She'd appear in knitted suits in jazzy colours. Her husband, Marty, was dedicated to handball and at their house on Malibu Beach, a handball game was always going on. Thinking back, for a woman so dedicated today to the well-being of stray animals, I never once saw Doris with a dog or a cat.

While making *Arabella* (1968) I had a most unnerving experience in a Rolls-Royce. On location in Italy, I was sitting in the back of this Rolls being driven to the beach at Ostia, where we were filming. I was idly thumbing through my script when I realized the car was doing something it ought not to be doing. It was slowing up in the middle of the busy highway. Soon, it would stop altogether. Cars were hurtling past us at a fine lick.

I leaned forward and looked at the Italian driver, sitting close to the wheel. But he didn't notice me, how could he? His eyes were closed. I shouted through the glass partition, but got no response. Eventually, I was able to force open the door. I got out. Dodged a passing car. Ran round the smoothly rolling Rolls. Climbed in the driver's side. Pushed the sleeping Italian over. And within a matter of seconds I had steered to the side of the road, put on the brake and turned off the engine.

I shook the driver, but got no reaction. So then I gave him a jolly good slapping about the face and gradually, life came back. It turned out to be just a case of his having over-eaten at lunchtime. I made sure that man never drove me again.

The death of a leading Italian actor just before shooting had commenced on *Arabella* had led to my being offered his rôles in the film – all four of them. It was a challenge to attempt four character rôles in one film. With the help of wigs, moustaches and lashings of Max Factor, I felt I easily conveyed those four different people without characteristics overlapping.

They were a neurotic hotel manager in a fuzzy black wig, pince-nez and a pale green face. A ginger-headed army general with a red face, ginger moustache and a monocle. A bland bank manager. And a blond-haired Italian count.

It all turned out beautifully. When the subject of billing came up, I was told that I couldn't have star billing because

James Fox, who co-starred with Virna Lisi, had a contract stipulating that the biggest billing must go to him. To get round this, they gave me four separate credits in the titles. This was a very effective ploy and many people in Rome had the impression that not only had I acted in the film, but that I had produced and directed it as well.

Virna Lisi and her husband had an elegant little yacht which they anchored at Ostia. I was invited to lunch one day, and to my horror, the waiter threw all the garbage into the sea. Remnants of spaghetti and lasagne were scraped from our plates over the side of the yacht and fell amidst swimmers.

I made a terse remark but Italians did that sort of thing everywhere. You just couldn't get them to see there was anything wrong in it.

Trevor Howard normally did a lot of laughing. But he didn't laugh at being kept waiting all day, until a quarter past five, to shoot his scene in *The Bawdy Adventures of Tom Jones* (1976). I thought it was very bad form to keep a star of his stature hanging around, and being Trevor Howard, he understandably filled in the time by having a few drinks. When he came to do his scene, he was blind drunk. He had to walk through a door and say, 'Ah!', waving his arm in the air. He did it so violently, he threw himself off-balance and hit the ground with a crash.

On the first day of filming *Seven Times Seven* (1969) on location in London's Jermyn Street, Sharon Tate came up and introduced herself. She said, quietly, 'I must tell you something before we start working together. I can't act, but I somehow get by without anyone realizing, so don't worry.'

Actually, Sharon turned out to share a distinction with Lena Horne – they were the only two performers I ever knew who were entirely 'natural' before the camera. Everybody else, method actors (and T-T too!) automatically took on a different stance and manner, as soon as the cameras started rolling.

So there were no difficulties with Sharon. We were like a

double act. She was nice, intelligent and pretty. I wish I had been able to see the finished film. I've never been able to catch it.

One that I didn't care whether I saw or not was *The Hound of the Baskervilles* (1978) with Dudley Moore and Peter Cook. I played the doctor. Paul Morrissey, the director, went on record as saying that comedy was completely experimental and had no rules. According to him, you could do anything that came into your head. As everybody's idea of comedy varied, this version of *The Hound of the Baskervilles*, consequently, made little sense.

It was, in fact, the most outrageous film I ever appeared in. From very early on I could tell that there was no magic, that it wasn't going to be very good. And it wasn't!

After seeing some rough-cuts, I left the studio with a clear opinion about the *Hound*. In technical language, it was bad! I should have got out of the business before ever agreeing to do it.

Which reminds me of the time I was doing a play for BBC television. I knew on the first day of rehearsals that it was hopeless. The director was pleasant, but he was doing nothing to try to improve things.

So I phoned Clive Nicholas, my partner and agent, and said, 'We're in trouble, boy. I need you over here as quick as possible. Just walk into the studio at Tottenham Court Road and say, "I'd like to speak to Mr Terry-Thomas. Would he join me at the White Elephant for lunch?"'

Over lunch, I told Clive that it was a very poor play and it would be bad news for us if I did it.

'Well, that's simple,' Clive said. 'Don't go back.'

So I said, 'Just like that?' He said, 'Yes, I'll handle it.'

So he came with me to the rehearsal room where the director said, 'What ho' to Clive. 'How are you, etc?' while I excused myself. Then Clive said that Terry-Thomas would not be returning to rehearse that afternoon, or for that matter, at any time.

And it *was* as simple as that. Instead of spending a few

unpleasant weeks mucking about in a rotten play, I went to the South of France. It was a breach of contract, of course, but they didn't do anything about it.

I should have done the same with *The Hound of the Baskervilles*. Why Cook and Moore continued with it, I have no idea. It must have been painfully obvious to them too, right from the very beginning, that the film stank.

6 Hi Hollywood! Hello Belinda

By 1960, I had stopped being a stand-up comic and definitely decided that my whole professional future was bound up in the world of films. Film-making had become my favourite medium. I suppose I had been in love with films since my days as an 'extra'. I adored the atmosphere, the smell, the noise and the tea (although I did not drink it, of course!) Though I owed so much to television, I felt that one could be seen far too much on the small screen and I'd more than had my fill. In the future, I determined, I would limit my appearance to the occasional television play. But as for radio and TV variety – never again. It was the cinema for me, and me for the cinema! I had already made my mark in British films. The next step was Hollywood.

Bachelor Flat was my first film there. But my initial experience in Tinsel Town could have put me off the place. No sooner had I arrived than I was 'pinched' by an agent called Mitchell Gerts. On behalf of the film company, he met my plane and took me to his apartment for food. I didn't need food and I was shocked by the size of the steaks that he prepared. He ate six.

I said, 'Mr Gerts. If you go on like this, you'll be dead in a very short space of time.'

'Oh, there's nothing wrong with me,' he said. And banged his stomach hard to show how strong and solid he was. He then claimed to be my agent. It was the first I'd heard of this. He had no right to represent me and I found it rather embarrassing. I wasn't particularly keen on agents anyway.

After a few days, I told the casting director of 20th Century-Fox that I was not at all happy that Mitchell Gerts had 'pinched' me. The casting director telephoned the head of the studio and said, 'Terry-Thomas has complained that Mitchell Gerts is posing as his agent.'

'You had better do something about it,' the studio chief replied.

A few days later, the chief called the casting director and said, 'When I told you to get rid of Mitchell Gerts, I didn't expect you to use such violent tactics. Mitchell Gerts has just died.'

Mitchell had died of over-eating, just as I said he would. All this happened within a few days of my arriving in Hollywood.

I had known only two other men as capable of sinking such vast quantities as Mitchell. One was the late King Farouk of Egypt. I once noticed him sitting on a stool in George's Bar, in Rome. Even from the back it had to be Farouk. How could one mistake that gigantic expanse of back-side? Queen Juliana and Prince Bernhard of the Netherlands were also dining, so was Fred MacMurray and his wife, June Haver. I wonder if they counted, as I did, the amount of stuff that Farouk ate. He calmly worked his way through twenty-two lamb cutlets, amongst other things, and finished with seven syllabubs.

Then there was impresario Henry Sherek. He was over twenty stone in weight and delighted in going to Simpson's in the Strand. He would clear an enormous amount of roast beef, carved from the joint at the table, by a team of men, then hand out sixpences as tips, rather as if he were feeding chickens.

Henry never drank alcohol of any sort because he said it affected his performance when making love.

Gluttons for food were rare, though, in Hollywood.

Everybody was diet-conscious and rationed their intake. Their food intake, that is. Drink was another matter. A lot of people did a hell of a lot of drinking. Far more than they did in Britain. More Martinis were ordered than anything else. Tequila was also popular and something called a French '78, named after a gun used in the Napoleonic Wars. It had been a most effective gun! The cocktail – champagne, brandy and rum – was pretty lethal, too!

I was invited everywhere, but I didn't enjoy it a lot. People drank far too much at a hell of a rate. By the time dinner was served, everybody except me was sloshed. I was stunned, not sloshed! This was invariably the case and I found it hard work keeping up.

Nearly everybody on my first film was the same. It proved to be contagious because, after a while, all the drinking got to me. Up to then I had been a very modest drinker. But for several years, in Hollywood, I wasn't even remotely sober. I soon realized that if one wanted to retain one's sanity there, one had to cut out 98 per cent of parties. The remaining 2 per cent were one's own fiestas.

Socially, Hollywood had its pecking order. People who were professionally in a different stratum of society did not get invited to certain parties. I disregarded that snobby rule and invited everyone I liked to my modest shindigs, irrespective of their jobs. I asked some cameramen, for example, and some little-known actors. To my astonishment, someone told me I was considered a bit of a freak to be so generous to people who were not in my class.

When I look back, I am amazed at the shabbiness of my behaviour during that period. We had tequila parties with quite lethal drinks. I used to go into restaurants blind drunk. Yet my constantly plastered state did not stop me from driving. In retrospect, I'm very surprised that I didn't have the most appalling accidents. Yet even though I was hitting the bottle, I was never late on set in the mornings.

Jack Lemmon was an inhibited drinker and I said to him once, when we were shooting a scene in a bar, 'You talk a lot about drinking, Jack, but you hardly drink at all. *You're inhibited*! I think it would be very much better if you just had whatever you felt like drinking, and not restrict yourself. I'm sure you wouldn't come to any harm.'

And I ordered a couple of large ones! In the shortest space of time, we really got stuck into dry Martinis, and it was the best filming that we had done.

While scenes were being lit, Jack played great jazz on the set and sang, to keep people amused. I liked that. What got on my nerves was his noisy way of winding himself up before he started on camera. He used to say, 'It's a fern. It's a fern. It's a fern.' Then he'd call, 'What is it, folks?' And the crew had to shout back, 'It's the magic hour.' Don't ask me what it meant. It was always the same ritual and it used to make me mad. My own technique to get myself going was quite different. I just used to jump in the air and execute a few dance steps ... but quietly.

Hollywood had everything for me. I liked it and I fitted into the scene. There were wonderful hotels, fabulous restaurants, incredible gardens.

The gardens were exotic and beautifully kept. Every foot of ground, wherever one looked, was cultivated. There were palm trees all over the place, bougainvillea, banana trees ... hibiscus. Landscape gardening was a most lucrative profession there. Lawns were so clipped and manicured and cared-for, they always seemed the same, as though the grass never grew any longer. There was no water problem which seemed a bit odd as it, literally, never rained. Apparently, all the water came from an abundantly wet State above California, and wherever one went, one saw water flowing and sprinklers doing their work.

Swimming pools were fairly conservative in construction, usually a straightforward rectangular or kidney-shape. There was not much statuary about – thank goodness. In the main, they were plain, functional pools with no fancy tiles. With all that sunshine, people spent as much time in the garden by the pool, as they did indoors.

Coming from Britain, I missed open spaces. All I saw was one empty field of about six acres, between Beverly Hills and Hollywood. It had been bought years before by Mary Pickford and Douglas Fairbanks, who had intended to build a house but never got round to it. That scruffy field was worth millions of dollars.

I had always loved walking, but it was very difficult to be a pedestrian in Bel Air or Beverly Hills. If one went for a walk, one would be picked up. The police patrol would want to know where one was going and where one had come from. And why one was on two feet and not in a car. I wasn't put off, and continued to walk everywhere.

Strolling down Rodeo Boulevard in Beverly Hills, I noticed that each road was lined with different trees, mulberries and so on. A Mexican gardener was doing his stuff near one that I couldn't identify and I said to him, 'I wonder if you could tell me what this is?'

He looked at me with a strange, scornful expression, then said, slowly and deliberately, 'It's a *tree*!'

I found very early on that people in Hollywood did say the most extraordinary things. Being fitted at Western Costumes once, a little man came into the changing room and dropped some clothes on the floor. 'These should fit you. I've seen you on TV,' he said.

'Oh,' I said. 'So this is the way you measure, by looking at people on the TV.' I pointed at the shoes he had put out for me. 'I told you I needed a size 11,' I said. 'Without trying those on, I can tell you they're a size 8.'

He then came out with this immortal line: 'Don't worry, I'll give them a bit of a polish.'

The quality of food in Hollywood restaurants was excellent. Yet a lot of eating places were as phoney as hell. Embarrassingly phoney. The waiters were constantly putting on the dog. They would talk rubbish about wine and go to great lengths to show off as they served it. I tried to discourage them by being more phoney than they were. I sniffed the wine, rubbed it on the palm of my hand, then *listened* to it.

Edie Adams had recently been widowed when we met on the set of *It's a Mad Mad Mad Mad World*. Her husband, comedian Ernie Kovacs, had crashed his car a few yards from their home.

The car had skidded sideways against an electricity pole and Ernie, thrown from one side of the car to the other, had hit the pole with his head and died instantly. Edie became my closest friend. For about a year we did everything together. Everything!

She was crazy, a most entertaining bird, though she used such strange jargon that, to a normal person, she was practically incomprehensible. Very often we'd be talking and I would gradually realize I didn't know what the hell she was on about. She mixed musicians' patter with psychiatric phrases and 'hip-talk'. She had picked up this grotesque style from Ernie, whose English had been very complicated indeed. He had been a man with strange ideas about life in general, and also a heavy drinker. Edie herself, then about thirty-two years old, was a big tippler, too.

I remember one night we went to Dean Martin's for drinks, called in at Jack Lemmon's house, then decided to take off on our own.

We went to the most formal restaurant to dine. The waiters wore tails and the floor was covered with full-sized Persian carpets. Edie was tiddly and I was sloshed, and feeling a bit facetious, I was in a mood to do anything.

Our waiter seemed so stuffy that I started playing a little game with him. I must admit I was out to make things as difficult for him as I could. I slid noiselessly to the floor, and Edie followed. When the waiter came to take our order, we sat there looking up at him and ordered shrimps, avocado pears, quiche Lorraine – and I think I also had a Wiener schnitzel.

There we were, Edie in a black, off-the-shoulder gown and I in a dinner jacket. And it just seemed very important that we should stay on the floor.

Our drinks arrived – I'd ordered a couple of French '78's –

but the head waiter looked as if he was about to put a stop to our fun and games. I quickly slipped him a big dollar bill and it worked like a charm. Well, there is something charming about a fifty-dollar bill, isn't there? Yes?

As the waiter brought our food, I lifted everything down from the table and we set it out, with great finesse, on the carpet. It was picnic time. I was thoroughly enjoying myself, and so was Edie. She kept giggling, 'Terry, you're so immaculate.'

Considering how her husband had so recently met his end in a car-crash, it was quite outrageous of me to drive her home in the state I was in that night. How I managed to do it remains a mystery. We were both reeling. But we got there.

She led me into a room that was full of electrical gadgets rigged up by Ernie. He had installed, for example, a complicated intercom system to all parts of the house, which was set in a big, old-fashioned desk with an arch in the middle. When you pressed various buttons, Ernie's recorded voice was heard giving instructions and directing you to different rooms. That dead man's voice barking out messages in the small hours was nightmarish.

Edie and I had some more French '78's, and it was not long before we were on the floor again ....

Edie gave me a watch that had belonged to Ernie with the figure 5 at each place on the watch-face where 1 to 12 should have been. This signified that, whatever the time of day, it was always cocktail hour.

I found the ultra-politeness of people on the telephone in America a sharp contrast to the rudeness of the taxi-drivers. One came across the most incredible rudeness and I determined from the beginning that I wasn't going to put up with it. At the slightest sign, I gave the chap a lecture. We didn't have to endure that sort of thing in Europe and I didn't see any point in allowing people to be rude to me for no reason at all.

Not that I often had to use taxis because in May, 1962, I imported a £9,500 Bentley Continental from Britain. On either side of the car I had two metal plates fitted, painted with the Union Jack, a small touch of patriotism that appealed to me and, at the same time, left no doubt as to whose car it was. Not that there could be much confusion because it was the only car of its kind in Hollywood: it was a right-hand drive! I never got it back after it was stolen in 1969.

I had various homes during my ten-year period in Hollywood. Sometimes I rented a house and other times I put up at the Beverly Hills Hotel, or at the Château Marmont where many famous artistes stayed. Sir Cedric Hardwicke lived there at the same time as I, and we got to know each other well. He was forever chatting to me about England and cricket. Once, I even played cricket with him. Cedric told me that since he had been knighted, he had been paying sir-tax.

What with films on both sides of the Atlantic and the same with TV, I didn't have very much time to do anything but exercise in the pool and go swimming at Malibu. Some friends of mine had houses there. Dorothy Carliss (Carol Carr's sister) was one. She had married a TV man, given up her career as a singer and moved to Malibu permanently. I often used to pop in on her for a swim in her pool and also in the sea because there was a raft about a quarter of a mile out. A seal used to bask there on the raft and we got to know each other pretty well.

With so much work it was impossible to go mad socially, or have too many late nights though I did make a point of keeping up with my colleagues from Britain, people like Denholm Elliott, Lionel Jeffries, Stanley Holloway and Peter Sellers.

What amazed me about Brits who had moved to Hollywood was the ease with which they had given way to Americanization. There was hardly anybody who was not affected. While making a point of being proudly British, they seemed unaware that American slang had seeped into their conversation. I hated Americanisms in speech. How they got on my nerves!

I was forever complaining to people and getting annoyed about it. Lionel Jeffries was one who, I thought, had become exceedingly American. He lived in American style in an American house and adopted all the well-known substitute words: elevator for lift, sidewalk for pavement, and so on. I remember taking him to task for using the expression to me: 'Were you laid last night?' I thought the boot was on the other foot and that, if anything, it should have been: 'Did you lay anybody last night?' When addressing a man, it seemed to make much more sense.

James Mason and his wife, although they had left Britain some years before, had remained ultra-British. Pamela, especially, was still incredibly Mayfair. I spent quite a bit of time with them in their very pleasant house. The food they served was excellent. Once, when I dined with them, I ordered my steak black on the outside and red in the middle, not thinking for a minute I'd get it. But I did. I would not have thought that their chef, whom they had flown over from the north of England, would have known how to cook a steak like that, but he certainly knew his onions.

Zsa Zsa Gabor was there that night – the most-painted woman I ever blinked at. Her then-husband, George Sanders, should have accompanied her, but they had quarrelled. They were always having rows; theirs was a very, very sad story. I was personally sorry that George hadn't turned up because he could usually be persuaded after dinner to play the piano and sing. He sang ballads awfully well, in a Noël Coward sort of way.

George and I had a good rapport because he had done his apprenticeship in revue before becoming a straight actor, so we had a lot in common. I didn't realize he drank so much until the day I went into a restaurant at Elstree and sat down at his table. We hadn't been chatting long when a boy came up to him and said, 'Mr Sanders, you're wanted on the set.' George got up to get his bill and I said, 'Don't bother, I'll settle it.'

When it came to paying, it was for far more drinks than I

had envisaged. So I said to the waiter, 'Surely Mr Sanders didn't drink all this just now, did he?' And the waiter replied, 'Oh yes. He always drinks quadruple vodkas, plus a dash of tonic water – about a saltspoonful!'

The only un-English aspect of James Mason's household were his two children, Morgan and Portland, who made a hell of a noise and argued a lot. Portland was an all-American girl, quite outrageously precocious. She had worn make-up and high-heeled shoes almost as soon as she could toddle. Meanwhile, young Morgan, at ten years old, had a great aptitude for billiards. I had several games with him and, with no effort at all, he beat me every time.

I used often to meet Dame Gladys Cooper in the very private bar they kept for VIPs at Los Angeles airport, an elegant bar behind a shabby-looking door. It looked like a loo-door. But inside, there was a splendidly luxurious room and bar, free to VIPs. Dame Gladys lived in a house near the airport. It suited her to be near as she was always travelling backwards and forwards by plane. I don't know how she stood all that travelling at her age. She had rather large feet and I used to joke that her feet came on to the stage first and then the rest of her followed a bit later on. That always made her laugh.

Michael Wilding was a cavalier, always escort to a succession of beautiful women, including his co-stars. When he made *Under Capricorn*, with Ingrid Bergman, Michael often took her to the Nightingale Club, in London, and I'd join them. The three of us would bash the brandy together. Then Ingrid and I would dance, usually the quickstep and the slow foxtrot. She was a big woman, as tall as I was – 6ft – and a good dancer.

In Hollywood, I used to meet Michael regularly in late-night restaurants, inevitably accompanied by Marlene Dietrich, with whom he had made *Stage Fright*.

It was always amusing to come upon Marlene, because she was so delightfully giggly.

Though charming and very good-looking, Michael was a

mass of nerves. Once, I saw him through a window when I passed a studio back-lot. I thought I'd go in and see how he was getting on. But by the time I got inside, he was on the set and had gone to pieces for some reason or other. He couldn't speak. When he tried, just a scrambled sound came out. It was a terrible thing to see someone who was a good performer just bumbling away, unable to perform at all. I slipped away so that he wouldn't spot me....

I'll tell you another anecdote about a Brit in Hollywood for no reason other than that it was so preposterous. I was in the grounds of the Beverly Hills Hotel when playwright Sir Terence Rattigan called me from his bedroom.

'Come up for a glass of champers, Terry,' he said.

His bed was by the window and it was obvious that he was in it. I asked him, 'Why are you in bed at this time of morning? What's the matter with you?'

'It's rather complicated,' called Terence, 'I don't want to spoil your day, but I have something wrong with me caused, so they tell me, by an impounded turd.'

I said, 'You shouldn't be lying in bed then. You should be riding.'

'Riding what?' asked bachelor Terence.

I said, 'Don't be facetious. How's your mother?'

'Oh,' he said. 'She's fine. How's yours?'

The last time I had seen his mother was during a cricket match at which Terence had been batting against a peer of the realm whose butler was acting as umpire. The aristocrat had had quite a bit to drink and his reflexes were slow. The ball came whistling down the field and hit him on the pad.

'Howzat!' shouted the bowler.

And the peer's butler said in a tactful, dignified voice, 'His lordship is not in.'

Talking about butlers, dining with Edward Everett Horton was quite an event. His butler used to supervise the evening meal with great aplomb, though I always had the impression the food had not been prepared in the kitchen but that someone had nipped round the corner to the nearest drugstore, and bought it ready-cooked.

After we had had the soup, the fish and/or the turkey, Edward's Cadillac would be brought round to the front door and we'd all pile in and tootle off to a restaurant for dessert. Then after our puddings and ice-creams, we would drive back to his home, take our same places at the table and resume conversation over coffee and brandy.

Edward was a pure eccentric, he didn't muck about. In the colossal lounge of his crazy house on the freeway, out of Vine, he used to burn furniture in the largest fireplace I had ever seen. Hanging by chains from inside the chimney stack was a huge metal net big enough to take sofas and divans and anything else that happened to be lying around. Edward considered he had amassed too much furniture, so he was gradually burning it up.

To make some cosy flames, Edward and the butler would heave piece after piece of furniture into the fire. Some of it could have been sold for a great deal of money. Come to think of it, Liberace would probably have been delighted to buy it because he had a couple of second-hand furniture stores (which he described as antique shops)!

So you see, I was certainly not the only alleged eccentric, there were lots of us about. In fact, most people in Hollywood struck me as being a bit weak in the top storey somewhere.

I remember the very first time I heard myself described as an eccentric, I wasn't at all pleased. Ted Kavanagh of ITMA came up to me and said, 'It's nice to have you as a member of the club because we were running short of eccentrics.'

I didn't like it, indeed, I was hurt and shocked. I didn't realize then that one could hardly use long black cigarette holders, peer through a monocle and wear fancy waistcoats and not be regarded as an eccentric. When I sat down to analyse myself, I agreed that sartorially I was an eccentric. But I knew that underneath the clothes I was very much a conservative Englishman who would have loved to have been a genuine eccentric.

Sex in Hollywood was easy to indulge in. For one thing, everybody made sure they looked fit and attractive always and there were lots of beds and divans available everywhere. It was not just boy-and-girl sex. For no reason that I can give, some of the toughest men in films suddenly 'came out of the closet' and let it be known that they were far more interested in fellows, to help them through the boring hours between midnight and dawn, than ladies.

My gentleman's decorum prevents me from mentioning the names of the daring, virile young bloods (and the not-so-young ones) who went back at night to their boy-friends. But there were many of them. No wonder lots of their female colleagues sought solace from *their* own sex.

In the past the studios had been careful to keep the sexual deviations of their stars from the knowledge of the public. Several marriages of convenience (like Rock Hudson's) had been arranged by the studios in order to preserve the virile images of their hot-property, contract macho actors. Naturally, the studio lawyers made sure they tied up all loose ends so that the glamorous bride – usually a starlet anxious for publicity – would be unable to claim much alimony when the marriage was not consummated.

One famous hunk of beefcake I once appeared with impressed me with his exaggeratedly handsome boy-friends who used to wait around the set for him. A condition was, apparently, they all had to be more strikingly good-looking than he was. Where he found these Adonises was a well-kept secret.

It wasn't all sexual deviation, of course, especially with someone like Diana Dors around. Ever since she had appeared with me, aged about twenty, in *How Do You View?* people have been asking me what she was like. Well, she was intelligent, exceptionally pretty and jokey – in other words, smart in every way; a splendid person to be with. She was once given the title: 'Number 1 in Beverly Hills' which was pretty good going when you remember she was originally a Miss Fluck from Swindon.

When I first went to Hollywood, Di and I had an arrangement whereby we swapped homes when we happened to be on opposite sides of the Atlantic. We both managed to spend quite a lot of time flitting backwards and forwards across the water. So I lived in her house in Beverly Hills and she moved into my flat in Kensington. During a period when we were both in Hollywood at the same time, I moved in as her house-guest.

Her rented home was all on one level. Not much to look at but nicely appointed and furnished, with swimming pool, of course, and a garden fenced-in for the sake of the two children.

A nurse from Devizes was in charge of the children and virtually ran the household. There were so many toys and games about, and other things belonging to the children, there was hardly room for anything else. It was clear that sex-symbol Dors adored her kids.

She was into her second marriage but that was not going well. It was obvious to me that Dickie Dawson was not in love with her, though I think she was with him. When Dickie was in a rage, because he thought that Di was carrying on with someone, he seethed. He carried a gun with him and said it was intended for Di's boy-friend. The man he referred to had tactfully vanished. I was terrified. I'm not afraid of firearms as long as I have one in my hand too. But Dickie, with his black moods and rages, flashing that gun around, scared the daylights out of me. Diana and Dickie had lots of spectacular fights and once he turned her out of the house. But she was tough. She always came up smiling.

Even when they separated and Dickie moved out, I continued to be Di's house-guest.

It was difficult to define our relationship. We were certainly very friendly! I had a big brother sort of affiliation with her, I suppose. Or perhaps she regarded me as a lascivious uncle. I knew I wasn't her type but I tried not to let that bother me because she certainly was mine.

We used to go to parties together. One day a director said

to me, 'I hear you are staying with Diana Dors. I saw you on Sunday night at the party and you were apparently getting on very well with her.'

'Yes,' I said. 'We do get on well.'

The director remarked, 'I wouldn't have thought that Dickie Dawson would be too happy with that arrangement.'

And I said, 'If you're suggesting that there is hanky panky going on, I'd like you to bear in mind that Dickie is a friend of mine. And Di and I were chaperoned.'

'Of course,' continued the director, 'It's no business of mine…'

And I chipped in, 'It seems as if you are making it so.'

'Well,' he said, 'she *is* exceptionally pretty.'

'True,' I told him. 'But one important point is that there are certain things which a gentleman doesn't do. And there is something more vital which I always bear in mind. And that is that Dickie Dawson carries a gun. And he never stops flashing it!'

What I didn't say was that Diana Dors and I had such an understanding that she did not bother to cover herself if I happened to pop into her bedroom when she was having a bath. Or after she'd had her bath, for that matter.

To an outsider it certainly might have looked as if there was something between Di and me because we sometimes shared the same bedroom.

We had a lot of fun watching TV together in her bedroom. Diana never drank much but – as she wrote about me in *her* book – I very often had one or two tequilas too many. One or two? Ha ha. There were nights when it was too much of a fag to go back to my own room. So I just stayed where I was by her side.

I had been on good terms with her first husband, Dennis Hamilton, even though I had always been careful to watch my step with him. Dennis suffered from a condition which excited the nerves and made the sufferer liable to do anything. He could become violent in a second.

I remember driving north in my Jensen – on a straight mile

– and suddenly there appeared beside me Diana Dors' famous light-blue Cadillac with Dennis at the wheel. He was alone. We must have been doing 80 miles an hour, maybe more. Dennis leaned nonchalantly across to the left to wind the passenger window down and started chatting to me as if we were in a bar, having a drink. I was too petrified to say much. I kept my eye on the brow of the hill in front of us, praying to God that no traffic would come over.

Dennis said, 'I'll see you later. Where are you staying?'

Even if I had been staying with Princess Margaret, I doubt whether I should have known at that precise moment.

Through Diana Dors' son, Mark, I was 'related' to Liberace and also to Pamela Mason and Steve Allen.

We were god-mother and god-fathers at Mark's christening. (The god-mother, in case you were trying to work it out, was Pamela, of course!) You'll no doubt be amazed to learn that Liberace wore a perfectly normal dark suit for the occasion.

I once dined with Lee (Liberace) and a friend of his, in the pianist's flamboyantly decorated home and I got bored waiting for the meal to be served. The all-coloured staff could be heard creating a terrific racket in the kitchen. Some crisis had arisen – but I could not find out what had gone wrong.

It was a startling house with some beautiful, ostentatious things, but what most impressed me was Lee's friend's smart blue-and-white seersucker suit. Lee himself was looking nonchalant in slacks and shirt. He was relaxed and quite subdued, didn't keep smiling *all* the time. After dinner, which was eventually served, he played for us but he didn't light the candelabra on the piano. I suppose he only did that for special guests.

I was flabbergasted that night to find that Liberace had had framed and then lovingly hung on the walls of his house the diplomas he had received for taking part in Royal Command Performances. I tried to think where mine were and couldn't. I fear I'd probably scribbled telephone messages on the back of them.

Scoundrel? Me? Never! *School for Scoundrels,* 1960.

A production still from *How To Murder Your Wife,* with jovial Jack Lemmon and the voluptuous Virna Lisi, 1964. (*Cinema Bookshop*)

With Jerry Lewis in *Don't Raise the Bridge, Lower the River,* 1968.

Belinda and I honeymooning at Paguera, Majorca, 1963.
(*Terry Daum*)

Another 'funnymoon' shot, Belinda and I doing our sea routine.
(*Terry Daum*)

My coy look. No wonder
Belinda fell for me!
(*Terry Daum*)

Bungho! Who the *hell* was I
with? I don't remember . . .

Despite the opulence of Liberace's house, it was a joke compared with Dean Martin's. Dean lived in more style than anyone else I saw in Hollywood. Dean's butler was a real butler. His furniture was beautiful. The carpets over wood floors were absolutely right.

Yet it was opulent without being ostentatious. Dean (or maybe his wife) obviously had a great deal of taste.

Marriage was a strange business in Hollywood. People were always getting married and unmarried. Each time they seemed to have an unfailing optimism that this time it was going to work. Many marriages did seem to be going well, then you would pick up the newspaper and see that the couple were about to divorce. I've known couples in Beverly Hills who appeared as close as they possibly could be. Yet after some trifling little tiff, they walked off into the middle distance, never to see each other again. Richard Harris and his wife, for example. They lived nearly next door to me and whenever I saw them they always seemed united. Suddenly they split.

I myself found that love was unpredictable. Had Pat allowed me a divorce when I first suggested it, Lorrae Desmond and I would have been man and wife years before I got to Hollywood. As it was, when Pat eventually agreed to end our marriage, I wasn't sure what to do. Because by then, there was another girl in my life – Belinda.

In the spring of 1962, Pat divorced me alleging my desertion eight years earlier. I offered no defence. To celebrate our parting, and remembering only too well the dog-lead with which Pat had attacked Lorrae, I presented her with a long-haired dachshund named Pagliacci – to go with the lead! Pat appreciated the joke. She shortened the dog's name to Archie and had him for many years. She adored him. She used to tell people, 'Archie's my consolation prize.'

A couple of years before this, I had gone on holiday with Lorrae to Cala Ratjada, in Majorca, a place full of cheery people and pretty girls, a place that excited me tremendously.

We stayed at the Pension Miravista, run by a card called

Tony Wheeler who told stories and sang songs with a ukelele.

On a subsequent holiday I went back alone – and that's when fate stepped in. I arrived at crack of dawn, and the three young girls who had taken summer jobs with Tony Wheeler drew lots to decide who should get up early to meet me.

Belinda Cunningham, a colonel's daughter from Lincolnshire, lost – or won, whichever way you preferred to look at it. She told me later she had quite resented having to drag herself out of bed for a mere *comedian* she had never heard of. Belinda, who was twenty-one, did not interest herself in show business at all. She had never seen me on television, nor been to any of my films or read about me in a newspaper. She later told me that her attitude had changed as soon as she saw me. 'Coooooor!' she thought. In other words, she found me a bit of all right. As for me, well, I had always preferred blondes and Belinda had soft blonde hair and a pair of the bluest eyes I'd ever seen. Need I say more? She also had an infectious smile, charming manners and a gentle-voiced upper-class accent. Posh! I went overboard for her, even though her previous unawareness of the existence of T-T was a bit daunting to my ego.

When I went to pay my bill at the end of my stay, there was a whacking great charge for 'repairs to roof'. The only way that I had been able to get to Belinda's room at night, without everybody knowing about it, had been across an extremely fragile tiled roof. One time I had had to climb on to a car and up a wall to get there. I'm sure you are immediately wondering, Dearest Reader, why I bothered to go to such lengths to get to Belinda.

Why didn't I just use the door and not worry what people thought? The answer to that reminds me of some Irish sight-seers who went to the maze at Hampton Court and panicked because it was shut and they couldn't get *in*. Besides, I took things like precarious roofs in my stride at this time. It was a frightfully energetic period of my life. I regularly used to hang from rafters to stretch my body, then stand on my head to let the blood run the other way.

I returned to London quite dazzled by my holiday romance. At the end of the summer, I found myself unexpectedly free between films, so I decided to return to Cala Ratjada for a few weeks. Instead of going by air, I got out my old XK 150, which was then the best Jaguar to date, and motored like mad to Majorca.

I did not let Belinda know I was on my way. I preferred to imagine her delight at seeing me suddenly pull up in front of the Miravista. My arrival would come as a big surprise.

But the surprise was mine. Belinda was no longer there. As the holiday season was near its end, her job had expired. While I had been motoring down, she had been returning by train. We must have crossed paths halfway. Disappointed, I plonked the huge bouquet of flowers I had bought for Belinda in Palma, into the arms of the Miravista's ugly old Spanish housekeeper. 'They're for you, Señora,' I said. She kissed me on both cheeks. One kiss would have been too many!

It was a hell of a shock to me to find that Belinda had gone. Eventually, I managed to contact her at her mother's home in Lincolnshire and suggested that she hotfoot it back. But that didn't suit her plans.

I was bitterly disillusioned.

I decided to make the best of things now that I was there. Cala Ratjada was more sophisticated and lively than any other place on the island and there were still numbers of pretty good-looking girls around, well-connected ones whose photographs graced the William Hickey column in the *Daily Express* and Paul Tanfield's page in the *Daily Mail*.

One of them was a strikingly beautiful, long-legged blonde called Mrs Helen Greville-Bell, who had a little white house by the water's edge. She had reluctantly received a bit of sensational publicity a few years previously. Her elderly lover, Miguel de Primo de Rivera, the Spanish Ambassador at the Court of St James, had been named as the 'other man' in Helen's husband's divorce action. Under a cloud, Primo de Rivera had subsequently been recalled to Spain by General Franco.

In the absence of Belinda, her friend Helen willingly became my guide. We drove along the coast visiting people she knew and swigged cocktails in their elegant white villas in the pines. We swam and sunbathed on isolated beaches by day and, at night, Helen took me to cosy restaurants where we dined well and consumed large quantities of wine. Helen had a pleasant ritual which unfailingly turned me on. She would light my cigar for me by holding it over a glass of flaming brandy, staring steadily at me the whole time, with her mocking, dark-brown eyes. It was quite romantic, really. In fact, without going into details, we had a jolly good time together.

I expect it was the heady atmosphere of those balmy autumn days with Helen that made me agree to break the law when I returned to Britain in the Jag.

I smuggled a dog through customs.

Through Helen, I had met a girl called Phoebe who had acquired a café-au-lait Ibizenco hound during her vacation in Cala Ratjada. She planned to take her pet to England but could not bear the thought of being parted from it during the six-month quarantine period. She suggested that I took the dog through customs hidden in my car, not as a dare but *a straight-forward smuggle*.

As I was so well known, she reasoned, I would be above suspicion and able to get away with it. I wasn't at all keen on the idea, but Phoebe was very persuasive. She bullied me all the way from Barcelona, up through Catalonia and France to Calais where I was going to take my car on the air ferry to Lydd. At last Phoebe got me agreeing to do it.

This was the most serious crime I was ever guilty of. In the past, I had knowingly driven an unlicensed motor car and exceeded various speed limits. In Hollywood I was frequently 'driving under the influence of drink'. But I'd done nothing as serious as smuggling a dog into Britain.

On one occasion, when Pat and I returned from France, customs officers had pounced on her new handbag and asked if she had bought it abroad. Pat denied it was new in such a manner that put their backs up. They asked me where she had bought the bag and I said I didn't know anything about it. 'We think you must know,' they told me.

I then got heated and replied, 'Don't tell me I must know. I'm telling you that I *don't* know.'

Pat had to pay duty. It was obvious that the bag was a recent purchase and not British-made.

I had been furious with her afterwards for attempting to take an expensive handbag – bought in Paris – through customs without declaring it. Now here I was about to do something far worse in the eyes of the law – flout rabies control.

Not that I felt, personally, that taking the dog in was a serious crime. So many countries in the world did not – and still don't – agree with Britain about the importation restrictions of dogs and other domestic animals. Had I felt strongly about it, I would have refused to do it. Nevertheless, I was shaking with apprehension as we approached the French airport and stopped under a tree to hide the 'goods'.

Phoebe was going to go through customs in another car which had been driving behind me from Barcelona. She fed the dog some aspirin to make it sleepy, then placed it under the roomy dashboard of my car, covered with blankets and a cushion.

Both our cars were loaded on to the little plane. We fastened our seat belts. And up we flew across the Channel to England – and a heavy fine, if I were caught.

The customs officer recognized me, of course. I nearly died when he put his head through the window of my car, a few inches from where the sleeping dog was hidden. The customs man gave a big grin: 'And how do you *view*, Terry-Thomas?' he said. 'How are you? Where have you come from?'

Forcing myself to sound as casual as possible, I made a few jocular remarks. I was literally trembling from the effort of trying to control myself. Even though I had not yet developed Parkinson's Disease, I did have a sort of Parkinson's attack of shaking.

It all seemed to be going well when suddenly, the Ibizenco hound from under his blanket, let out a muffled, sleepy whimper. I thought the game was up.

'What's that?' asked the customs man as I quickly reached for the knob of my radio and flooded the car with static and noise. I made a feeble excuse about the radio not having worked before.

'Jolly good, it's come to life now we're back home. Loose connection, I suppose,' I blustered. 'Now I can have some music on my way to London. May I leave? I've got to hurry because I'm doing a show.'

Somehow I found first gear and revved away. Only afterwards, when I watched a gleeful Phoebe drive off with the dog, did I realize what an extremely wrong and foolish thing I had done. Had I been caught, it would have put me in a very awkward position.

I now had two steady girl-friends, Lorrae and Belinda. Although I had told Belinda about Lorrae on our first meeting in Majorca, it didn't seem necessary to tell Lorrae about Belinda. So I didn't. What with alternating between the two and frequently whizzing back to Hollywood to do a film, my life was full.

It was about this period, when I was crossing the Atlantic as many as twenty times a year, that I started taking my own food with me for the journey. I had found that I was losing weight with the indigestible food the airlines served in first class. So I embarked with a zip-up picnic box ice-cooled and packed with succulent everyday goodies like Russian caviar, pâté, smoked salmon, cold chicken, cream cheese, Brie, potted shrimps, salad, water-cress, brown bread and mineral water. Oh, and some hand-made chocolates.

You could get most of these things in first class, but I

preferred my own. At first I was terribly embarrassed and used to say that I was orthodox Jewish when I handed my picnic box to the stewardess to keep for me until mealtime. 'This is something specially prepared by my own rabbi,' I'd say, with an apologetic cackle.

When I stopped being embarrassed, I'd also take lamb cutlets which I got the steward to cook for me. My partner and lawyer, Clive Nicholas, entered into the spirit of my picnic preparations and got his wife to contribute the odd bonanza, like angels-on-horseback (oysters wrapped in bacon).

So why go first class, you're wondering, when the only benefit I got was more leg-room? That was the reason! I had rather long legs – still have, as a matter of fact – and didn't want to be squashed up on a transatlantic flight.

When I travelled on a Jumbo – and I tried to as often as possible – my preparations increased. I took my own wine with me and my own flower arrangement for my table. I despised that formal set arrangement of gladioli, chrysanthemums and carnations on a shelf that inevitably greeted you on entering the plane. Though real, those flowers looked so plastic. To brighten my journey, I used to take a small posy of violets, picked from my own roof garden, or some lovely bit of blossom pinched from Kensington Gardens or Hyde Park. That was a little crime of mine: nicking cuttings and flowers, after dark, from one of the public parks or gardens.

Lorrae went back to Australia for a while, then flew over to visit me in Hollywood when I was making *The Wonderful World of the Brothers Grimm*. At the time, I was staying at the Château Marmont and naturally booked for her to share my suite, which was our normal arrangement. For some reason, this made her furious. She flew into a rage when she was shown to my room and demanded a room of her own. Perhaps that little scene was the first time I realized that we were not getting on as well as we had in the past.

By now, the strain of running two romances was affecting my nerves. I was seeing Belinda regularly in London and getting more and more involved with her. We had even talked casually about marriage. But Belinda insisted that she would not marry me unless she became pregnant. She wanted to be sure she was capable of bearing a child before tying herself down to matrimony. Over a couple of years, she spent lots of nights with me, and we certainly tried hard to put her in the family way. Great fun – but nothing happened!

Emotionally – and physically – I was still strongly attached to Lorrae, even though we were always on the move and were separated a great deal of the time. Over the years, Lorrae had come to mean a great deal to me. I was in the unsatisfactory position of loving them both: Belinda, who was twenty-six years younger than I, and Lorrae, who was my junior by eighteen years.

When Lorrae returned to Australia following her trip to Hollywood, I knew that the time had come when I would have to choose between them, once and for all. For years Lorrae and I had taken it for granted that we would marry when my divorce eventually came through. And I was now divorced. It was only fair to her – and to Belinda – that something must be decided. I didn't know what to do.

It was Belinda's idea that I should go out to Australia to visit Lorrae and help me reach a decision. It must have been heart-rending for her to unselfishly suggest such a move as it could have brought about the end of our relationship. I knew she was deeply in love with me. She just couldn't bear to see me growing so wretched due to my dilemma.

I had to assess the situation and balance the advantages of one pretty bird against the other. So I kissed Belinda goodbye and flew off to wildest Australia.

By now, with all her international experience, Lorrae had developed into a marvellous performer. Lovely figure, good stage presence, strong voice – she had everything. Yet after a few weeks with her, I knew with a sinking heart that it would never work between us. We did not gel as well as we had before. When she had lived in England, she had appeared to be very English. But back in her own country, I noticed that she was typically Australian. And I didn't like her so much that way.

I remember leaving her for the last time in Sydney. It was late at night. I told her I would be returning immediately to Britain. It was over between us, I said. It was clear to me that we would never make a go of it. Lorrae said in a quiet voice, 'But I thought, Terry, we were going to be married.' And I said, 'No! I'm quite certain that it would not be a good idea.'

In a way, I got the impression that Lorrae was relieved. I knew she had a boy-friend in Sydney, a brain specialist. She had introduced me to Dr Alex Gorshenin in a restaurant. He seemed a nice enough chap and was obviously very interested in Lorrae and she in him.

On the long flight home I was filled with mixed feelings. Remorse took over from relief and vice versa; nevertheless, I was certain that I had made the right decision. Of course I was sad because it was the end of an era for me. Lorrae and I had had some wonderful times together over the last ten years. I knew I still felt very deeply for her. I still found her incredibly attractive and I knew she was probably the most highly sexed woman I would ever meet.

When I read in the paper, a few months afterwards, that Lorrae had married Dr Gorshenin, I went to pieces. Why I broke down and wept, I don't understand. After all, it had been I who had finished our affair. I'd been the one who had decided against our getting married. But knowing she was now another man's wife made the ending so final. I felt betrayed.

That's when Belinda stepped in and nursed me back to health. She moved into my flat and I got better with her love, her care and her understanding.

But she still wouldn't marry me. Not until ... or unless she was going to have my child.

7   *Ibiza*

I came off the set of *It's a Mad Mad Mad Mad World* in Yucca Valley, and thought I would telephone Belinda for a chat. I put in a transatlantic call. 'Hello Terry,' said Belinda from London, sounding as if she were just down the road. 'You'd better buy the house next door; we'll need the extra room. I'm preg!'

I stared at the phone in astonishment. After all this time, after five years, I was going to be a dad, at last. I was terribly thrilled and a bit staggered at the news. I rang her mother and without thinking, shouted down the line, 'Isn't it marvellous! Belinda's going to have a baby.'

Really, I can be a bit of a Charlie at times. I had no idea that Nell would be pleased. She might have been horrified to know that I had got her unmarried daughter pregnant. I suppose I really should have been a teeny bit embarrassed at having achieved this.

But Belinda soon assured me that Nell, who had married again, already regarded me like a son-in-law and was happy for us.

We couldn't say the same about Belinda's father. Colonel Peter Cunningham had been so upset when he found that his daughter was 'carrying on' with a comedian as old as Belinda's mother and nearly as old as he was himself, that he had tried to break up the relationship. Belinda had been abruptly 'posted' to Singapore to a protocol job her father had arranged for her. He was serving there and he felt he would be able to keep an eye on her.

She worked for the naval chief of staff, a vice admiral, as his personal assistant and we did not see each other for ten months. But we kept in lively contact with lots of letters. Between making bright conversation at the endless cocktail and swimming parties she helped to organize, Belinda used to pop down the road to a village store run by Chinese friends of hers to use their gramophone and listen to me. I had sent her my first record album, 'Strictly T-T.'

Colonel Cunningham had to accept, when he knew about the baby, that he would soon have a comedian as a member of the family. In view of how things turned out I shall never forget one of the first conversations I had with him. 'Have you got any money?' he asked me. 'A bit,' I said, 'why?' 'Well, watch out,' said the colonel. 'My daughter will spend all of it if you give her a chance.'

When I got back to London, Belinda made me smile about the day her pregnancy was confirmed. She described the doctor as the double of James Robertson Justice. 'It's good news,' he told her with a kindly smile. 'You *are* going to have a baby, Mrs Cunningham.'

'How lovely! I'm so pleased!' said Belinda. 'But it's *Miss* Cunningham, not Mrs. I'm not married.'

The smile vanished from the doctor's face and as if he had not heard, he grimly continued to call her *Mrs* Cunningham throughout the rest of the conversation.

She moved into the flat again with me and we did a round of parties and shows. I took her to her first première. This was the first time she had been exposed to photographers' flash bulbs. She didn't take to it much. So when we married, she insisted on a completely private ceremony.

She knew the Press would find out eventually, but on The Day she wanted it to be just us. No family. Just two lawyer friends of mine to act as witnesses.

I was so easily recognized I had to adopt some sort of

camouflage, otherwise we feared someone might spot me, that August morning in 1963, escorting Belinda into Halstead Register Office, near Colchester, Essex.

It became a game with us 'to fool T-T spotters' as the *Daily Express* neatly put it when the news of the marriage leaked out eleven days afterwards. In readiness for my next film-rôle, as a naval officer in *The Wild Affair* (1963), with Nancy Kwan, I had had to shave off my moustache. Naval tradition decreed that officers had to have a full set (moustache and beard) or nothing. So having a naked upper lip helped a lot to change my appearance and I had a special denture made to fit the gap in between my teeth, my most obvious giveaway trademark.

Nobody found out. I wore grey suede shoes to go with my grey suit and silk waistcoat. As Belinda and I left the register office, man and wife, Clive Nicholas, my lawyer, said, 'I think we'd better scarper. I don't think the town has ever seen grey suede shoes before.'

Indeed, it was my shoes, not my face, which were attracting a bit of attention.

For our honeymoon we went back to Majorca. Not to Cala Ratjada where we had met, but to Paguera on the other side of the island. It was there that Terry Daum, co-author of this book, first caught up with me. He was based in Palma as a freelance journalist and came rushing for an interview when he heard that we had saved three English holidaymakers whose dinghy had overturned.

Belinda and I had been out on a pedal boat when we saw a red dinghy capsize. We became horrified witnesses as the crew of three, Mr and Mrs Edward Morgan and a friend, Mr Eric Wadham, all of West Wickham, Kent, were tipped fully clothed into the water. They immediately started thrashing about and making no end of a splash. Mr Morgan, a dry-cleaner by trade, was getting wetter and wetter. He shouted, 'Save my wife. Save my wife. She can't swim!'

Belinda and I pedalled towards them as fast as we could. Then we helped them to clamber aboard our pedal-boat and swam behind them as they paddled back to shore. There had been nothing heroic about it, anyone in similar circumstance would have done the same.

Two more near-drownings were to feature in my life. One day, in the swimming pool of a Cairo hotel, I had a bit of a split mind. I had a very strong feeling that a girl in the pool was in danger.

I swam up to Rod Steiger. (We were in Egypt making *The Heroes*). 'See that girl,' I said to him. 'She is probably about to drown.'

I pointed to a girl who was motionless and floating upside down on the water.

'My God!' said Rod and shot off with the speed of a shark. He got the girl out, gave her the kiss of life and brought her round. Afterwards he said to me, 'Why didn't you save her?'

'Well,' I said, 'You weren't doing anything and you look the sort of person who likes to save people. Besides, I wasn't in the mood.'

Steiger said later to Rod Taylor, 'Now I *know* that Englishman's crazy.'

In about 1981 I nearly drowned myself. In Ibiza, Belinda and I had been swimming in a quiet cove. We left the water and she went off to get a gin and tonic, leaving me sprawled on the sand. Something made her suddenly turn back before she reached the bar. She saw me struggling in the surf. I was floating upside down, obviously in trouble. She dived in and hauled me out.

That had been my own fault for attempting to swim alone. I had not taken notice of the booklet provided to sufferers of Parkinson's Disease which advises that one should never go into the water unless accompanied. It was a frightening way to learn a lesson.

Naturally the highlight of 1963 was my marriage, but the year sticks in my mind for a number of other reasons. That was the year of the Profumo affair, of course, with its huge cast of well-known characters. I was featured too, in a very modest way. When the ill-fated osteopath, Dr Stephen

Ward, had an exhibition of his portraits in chalk at the Museum Street Galleries, I was up on the wall with his other famous models, priced – with Nubar Gulbenkian – at 100 guineas. Mr Kruschev was hanging nearby, with a 150 guinea tag, Archbishop Makarios and Viscount Astor had 200 guinea tickets and Prince Philip and Princess Margaret were the prizes of the exhibition at 500 guineas each.

(Talking about the obsolete guinea reminds me of the old woman who was brought up before Judge Snell at Highgate police court. The judge said to her, 'So you were drunk?'

'Well your honour,' she said. 'It is not a nice word to use to a lady. I might have been inebriated or under the influence of alcohol but I certainly wasn't *drunk*.'

'Oh, I see your point,' said Snell. 'In the circumstances, I propose to fine you two guineas, instead of forty-two shillings.')

I had the honour of doing a sketch with Bing Crosby on TV that spring and also *The British at Play*, a series of sketches, by Stephen Potter, designed to throw light on Britons on holiday at home and abroad. Wendy Craig starred. It was an exciting challenge for me, which came off. I played a dozen different roles and loved it. For one of the parts, as a rustic, I worked on a battered old hat for a couple of days to get it to the condition I wanted. Eventually, I achieved the required look by pouring tea over the hat and baking it in the oven.

In April I appeared as the mystery guest on Eamonn Andrews' *What's My Line?* on BBC TV. After being identified, I confounded Eamonn and surprised viewers (myself too, I might add) by suddenly attacking the satire programme *That Was the Week That Was*.

I said, 'I saw that programme *That Was the Week That Was*, thank you. I have never seen anything like it. I was completely astounded.' The audience applauded me.

Warming to my theme, I criticized the 'instant fame' that television could now bring to what I considered 'untrained performers'. I then described Bernard Levin, as he appeared in 'that' programme, as 'a sort of kosher poor-man's Billy Graham'.

I don't really know why I made this spontaneous outburst, except that I wasn't feeling well. I had bronchitis and I had been embarrassed by the programme when David Frost had leered into the camera and told a story about a man who had been 'playing with himself'.

The BBC reported that nine viewers had phoned to complain that my remarks had been offensive. But I had no regrets about what I'd said.

A number of people suggested that this incident provoked the next one. It could have been. I shall probably never find out.

A few days after my marriage, I was attacked in *Private Eye*. A cartoon was published which quite clearly set out to prove a point. That although I was known to the public as an immaculately turned-out person, I was, in fact, the reverse.

I was shown twice. On a poster outside a theatre I was pictured healthy, happy and spotlessly dressed – as I always was. But beneath the poster, I was seen skulking out of the stage door bearing the look of an unshaven, unkempt, sleazy, run-down character sucking at a cigarette end.

I had no idea why I had been chosen as the subject of the cartoon, or why I had been treated in this way. I was extremely angry because I regarded it as a grossly impudent and unwarranted attack. I immediately issued a writ for libel against Pressdram Ltd., publishers of *Private Eye*; Leo Thorpe Ltd., printer; Barry Fantoni, cartoonist; Christopher Booker, Richard Ingrams, William Rushton and Brian Moore, all members of the editorial board.

At the first opportunity, *Private Eye* apologized in print. They freely admitted that I had the reputation of a highly respected actor and a clean figure of fun.

No attempt was made to justify the cartoon. Eventually, the magazine paid me damages – a few thousand quid – and in the High Court, before Mr Justice Phillimore, the record of my libel action was withdrawn.

The whole thing had caused a lot of upset, so it was gratifying to hear Mr David Turner-Samuels, for the defendants, say that no derogatory motive had ever existed. *Private Eye*'s case was, he said, or would have been, that although I was in fact a dapper, happy, lively, good-humoured and mirth-provoking actor, I was, like all other mortals, liable after the show to the emotions, irritations, worries and fatigue which beset everyone.

A few years later, another member of the family – well, an ex-member by then – was also to get a mention or two in *Private Eye* because of his involvement in 'the Jeremy Thorpe case'.

It never reached the Press at the time of the case (which led to the resignation of the Liberal leader) that male model, Norman Scott, whom Thorpe had once befriended, was a former brother-in-law of mine.

Norman had married Belinda's sister, Susan, rather against her family's wishes because he had been honest from the start about his homosexual tendencies.

'I don't think your family likes me at all,' Norman complained to Belinda. And she told him, 'Well, understandably, they're a little worried.'

I wanted to be as helpful as I could so Belinda and I gave them a rented cottage outside Taunton as a wedding present.

It seemed that the marriage was not a happy one and they cried a lot, but they did produce a smashing son, Benjamin. Unfortunately, Norman felt unable to cope with the extra responsibility and he scarpered when the baby was three weeks old. There was a divorce and Susan married a farmer.

Belinda was about six months pregnant when she first went to Hollywood to set up home with me, temporarily, at the Regency, a hotel with suites along the Sunset Strip. She liked it well enough but she was singularly uninterested in the Hollywood scene. I had never met anybody like her because her attitude to show business was quite unique. For instance, I took her to a theatre once and she talked in a loud voice about the performers as though they were animals.

Another time she accompanied me to a recording session and started chatting to me, halfway through a song, as though we were alone at home or walking in the park.

Soon after she arrived, a 'Welcome to Terry and Belinda party' was thrown for us by Bill Dozier, producer of a Hollywood TV series, a man who was very keen to get me. Fold-over matches saying 'Welcome', with our pictures printed on them, were handed to each of the 150 guests, some of the biggest names in Hollywood including gossip writers Louella Parsons and Hedda Hopper.

But as Belinda had never seen many films, or interested herself in the show business scene, she had no idea who the world-famous people were who came up and shook hands with her. She didn't recognize any of them and couldn't tell you today who was there. All she said to me was, 'They're a very glamorous crowd, aren't they? Some of them are *terribly* good-looking. And can't they drink!'

The party was the inevitable scramble with everyone free-loading just as fast as they could.

Belinda has always felt a bit guilty that her non-interest in stars made me more introverted than I already was. Being an Army daughter from a posh family, she was not impressed by my monogrammed shirts, for instance, and never stopped ribbing me about them. That certainly did something to my ego.

When I had started in show business I was very wild, but I changed. The knocks of life taught me over the years that I was not such an extrovert as I had thought I was. Quite the other way, actually. The late hours when I did cabaret had not helped. Sometimes I didn't get home until four or five a.m. and it did not suit me. By the time I got to Hollywood and had Belinda by my side scoffing a bit about my 'showing off', I was not keen to enter into idle chatter.

In The Daisy, a very exclusive club where one went to be seen and to observe, in turn, folks like Frank Sinatra lurking in the shadows, I hardly ever conversed with anybody other than the ones in my immediate party. When I used to see somebody I recognized, our eyes would meet and we'd have a little private smile as though we were superior to it all, and pass on into the night. I used the same ploy when I dined in a lovely Italian restaurant called Chasens which was always stuffed with big names.

Writer Rosemary Edelmann became one of Belinda's best friends in Hollywood and threw girls' parties for her at Malibu. Belinda quite enjoyed these even though some of the Hollywood women made her sad.

'They wear masses of make-up and look fantastic when the evening begins,' she said to me. 'But after their third drink, their faces crumble and harden and you see what they are really like.'

Mind you, she herself could knock it back – as I said before, it was catching – but she was young and had such a good English complexion there were no ravages in evidence on her face.

The night we were invited to dinner in Glenn Ford's most beautiful house behind the Beverly Hills Hotel, Belinda had to go up to Glenn and whisper that Terry didn't enjoy food without wine. Everyone else was drinking Martinis. So Glenn got a large bunch of keys and took me down to a cellar. I chose a Pommard '28 (a wonderful year!).

The wine was opened most ceremoniously by one of Glenn's staff and ... I could hardly believe it ... it was only a quarter bottle. Belinda had to go back to Glenn and say, 'Terry thanks you very much for the wine. It *is* the stuff he likes, so can he have some, please?' Next time I got a half-bottle.

I suffered a similar experience when Belinda and I went to dinner with Tony Curtis. It was an awfully boring evening because Tony, a terrific show-off, was also very, very mean. Eventually we had to ask him straight out if he would be so kind as to open the wine.

What I most remember about that evening was when he proudly showed us his 'boxes'. As a hobby he made boxes out of everything. There was even a Bible with its innards scooped out. The boxes were all rather sinister and, I thought, badly designed. The most extraordinary part was, he didn't put anything in them.

Belinda quite enjoyed Hollywood once she had accepted that artificiality was what the film capital was all about. Hollywood certainly enjoyed her because she was an eccentric in her own right. Hollywood folk could identify with that. I was the surprised one, I hadn't realized I had married an eccentric.

I recall Belinda getting up from a table where we were with friends, in a house in the Valley, and returning quietly, a few minutes later, dripping wet without a stitch on. 'Aren't you coming in?' she asked. 'It's lovely!'

That spontaneous sort of action of hers always broke the ice. And very pleasant it all was. There were several occasions when people bathed naked and if I was invited to use a pool and was in the mood, I accepted with alacrity. Like everybody else, I tended not to bother with swim trunks, they were such an awful nuisance. I suppose I took terrific risks. Rather foolish of me because some astute photographer might have snapped me starkers. But *Confidential* never got me!

We flew back to Britain only a couple of weeks before Belinda's confinement. I was interviewed by the *Evening News* which announced in big letters: 'Terry-Thomas is a father-to-be.' I told their reporter, 'It's all terribly thrilling, old man. Actually, we rather wanted a dog. But now we're hoping for a girl and I've been busy buying pink rattles and bells. We've been trying to think up a name that we both like – I've settled for Trilby, from "Svengali". Rather nice, don't you think? If it's a boy, we'll call him Timothy.'

A week later, we were getting concerned for the baby was overdue.

All along, Belinda had been in royal pregnant-mum company. I quipped in the *Daily Mail*: 'I thought she'd beat the Queen to it. Now I've told her there'll be trouble if she doesn't beat Princess Margaret.'

The baby had still not arrived when I had to return to America to begin work on *How to Murder Your Wife*.

When Timothy Hoar Stevens did make his appearance at the Princess Beatrice Hospital in London, four days later, I felt awful to be so many thousands of miles away from Belinda. Over the telephone I heard that all was not well with Timothy. His foodpipe had not been joined to his stomach and that had necessitated an emergency operation at the Queen Elizabeth Nursing Home for Children, at Hackney. He was crucially ill. It was a couple of weeks before he came off the danger list and a month before I could fly home to see him. Thank God all was well.

When Timothy (whom we'd nicknamed Tiger) was just a few months old, Belinda flew out with him to join me in America, just as Lorrae Desmond and her husband arrived in Hollywood on a visit. It was a bit disconcerting for Belinda who was still feeling awful, with post-natal blues and certainly not looking her best, to be confronted at last by 'this luscious girl, all curvaceous and gorgeous' (Belinda's description of Lorrae).

Belinda gamely faced the situation and the four of us sat up the whole night talking. I had got over Lorrae completely by then. I saw her simply as a very dear old friend, that was all.

I realized that when I had made my choice, though I was a very romantic person, I had let myself be guided by my intellect, not by my heart. I would never have thought I could have been so intelligent as to do that. But I did it and it had paid off handsomely. I felt terribly flattered that Belinda had married me.

We still have a good contact with Lorrae. As a matter of fact, only a few nights go, Lorrae, on a trip to Europe, stopped off to see us in Majorca, where I'm writing this book. She still looked smashing.

After supper, I asked her kindly to peruse the bits I had put in the book about her. A gentleman, officially, should never kiss and tell and I felt I might have been somewhat swinish in spilling the beans about our affair.

Lorrae chortled as she read through. Then she gave me a wide grin and silently mouthed one line of a song: 'Thaaaanks for the Memory.' So that was all right. She didn't mind my caddish behaviour.

She told us she had turned to drama and had successfully starred in an Australian soap opera, *A Country Practice*, which has also been seen in Britain. She had divorced in 1976 and now shared her home with a girl-friend and a lot of dogs.

I realize I had better fill you in as to how I came to be in Majorca, pen all a-quiver. Otherwise, Dear Reader, you are going to get frightfully puzzled and we can't have that happening.

When the debris of our divorce had settled, Pat and I eventually resumed a good friendship. After all, we still had so many memories in common and I was still very fond of her. As for Pat, right up to her death, aged eighty, in June 1983, she went on loving me very deeply.

She had settled in a delightful, two-bedroomed cottage in Majorca and I often used to telephone her for a chat, to ask her advice about something or other. She was a clever old thing and a good listener. Sometimes I popped in to see her.

To her credit she could have condemned Belinda but instead, over the years, they became very friendly. Indeed, Pat once invited Belinda to stay for a few days and I supposed they both had a jolly time talking about my failings, which they were both well acquainted with. Belinda had a great deal of affection for Pat and was nearly as sad as I was when she died.

I inherited Pat's little cottage, S'Olivera, which is set in the hills behind Palma with an absolutely splendid view of Bellver Castle. It is here during the balmy, Balearic winter months of 1983-4 that this book has taken shape.

But enough of the present. Let me reminisce ... 1957 ... that was the year I did a rather flippant article for *TV Times*.

'I want money to burn,' I wrote. 'I want to light a cigarette with a £5 note ... I'm not planning to burn money as a regular hobby, but talking strictly in terms of frivolous expenditure, it is after all, a fairly healthy way of squandering brass. It's all good, clean fun. When you come to think of it, there are worse ways. The only criticism that can reasonably be levelled at burning money is that no benefit will accrue to anyone else – as it might, for example, if I were to toss back £5 in drink, or make some bookmaker happy by putting it on a horse. By burning my money, I'd be having £5 worth of satisfying, albeit – on a time basis – expensive fun. It would be one glorious moment of abandon.'

During my Hollywood period 'burning money', or rather, squandering it, became the norm rather than just 'one glorious moment of abandon'.

The cost of living was high and one didn't hold back. What with entertaining, living expenses, exorbitant rents, staff and transport, I got through an alarming amount of the stuff very quickly. I was earning it, so why not spend it?

The stubs of my cheque books reveal that I got through millions of dollars, but where did it go? There's not much solid evidence to show for it today, apart from a few bits of property. A terrifying amount was wasted on clothes that were never worn. There were trunks full of expensive outfits that Belinda and I bought but never got round to using. There were so many shops handy and easy to get at, filled with tantalizing goods. Whatever Belinda and I wanted, we bought. And we wanted the lot. We knew the fat cheques in the pipe-line were endless.

Once, we rented a house in Bel Air for £2,000 a week. Standing back from the road, in a lush garden with palms and lots of camellias, there was an oblong swimming pool and a tennis court. A coloured girl and a chap looked after us. Looking back, though it was pleasant, there was nothing exceptional about it. It had not been necessary to get such an expensive house; I didn't *need* that sort of prestige. But why not?

When I spent a couple of months in Sydney, in the play,

Don't Just Lie There, Say Something, I did exactly the same thing. I got caught by someone overcharging. I couldn't find anywhere else decent, so I took a house with a guest-house, a pool and studio attached. All that cost well over £8,000 a month.

I had not been such a spendthrift until I met Belinda. She changed my life in that aspect. Most actors were terribly afraid of spending money. It was a kind of built-in caution. But Belinda would have nothing to do with that attitude. She had none of that insecurity. She made me relax and taught me that it was ridiculous to worry – the quickest way to get ulcers.

Having the means, I couldn't have stood a wife who sat on money, so if Belinda wanted something, she jolly well got it.

Once, I telephoned her from New York because a new project had been offered me. I said, 'Darling. If I stay another day, I can earn £4,000.' And she said, 'What do you want with another £4,000?'

What she meant was that she had some jobs for me to do around the house. I realized, of course, that having a dear wife as blasé as that about money, I ruddy well had to go on earning it.

When I made my first film in France, in 1966, Belinda was ill and couldn't go with me. So I commuted daily to Paris from Heathrow in order to be at home at night to cook dinner. This was regarded in the British Press as a most ostentatious gesture on my part. But was it, really? First class return fare from London was only £24.80 (or £24.16.0 as it was then). Hardly heady expenditure!

It was the money I earned for making commercials that made my bank manager smile. I could earn £10,000 a day and some of the contracts entailed a couple of weeks' non-stop filming. Yes, I agree it came to a lot of money, but it was jolly hard work and the advertiser did have the use of my voice and image for a long period. Also, it had been proved over and over again that Terry-Thomas was a definite boost to the sales of any product.

I once did an ice-cream commercial in Australia. It was simple, all I had to do was talk into camera. But it was so successful and sold so many extra ice-creams, I was asked to go back and do another one the following year when my fee was automatically doubled.

Nowadays everyone does commercials if they can, even members of the theatrical hierarchy. But once there was a stigma attached to lending one's face to endorse commercial products. It wasn't considered done! I never had any emotional problems about it. To me, it was another extension of the profession.

It was about thirty years ago that my office contacted me and said, 'Would you like to do a commercial for Mars bars?' I replied, 'If the money is interesting enough, I should be delighted.' I can't remember how much had been offered but it obviously satisfied me.

The chocolate firm's idea was to cash in on the gap between my teeth and show me close-up taking a bite out of a Mars. The trouble was, while I adored handmade chocolates, I wasn't keen on Mars. So as soon as the shot was over, I spat out what I'd bitten into a basin. Quite a number of shots were done, so a great deal of spitting went on.

When one of my colleagues rather snootily asked me afterwards why I had done the commercial, I said, 'Well, I've always wanted to play Shakespeare.'

It was a nonsensical reply, intended to mystify, and it did. Funnily enough, years later in a commercial for frozen fish, I was cast as the Bard himself. Bubbly June Whitfield was Anne Hathaway. At least that frozen fish ad enables me, truthfully, to say here, that I have played Shakespeare!

(Once, I nearly appeared in a Shakespeare play. I was offered the role of Prospero in *The Tempest*. 'Oh, yes please,' I said, jumping up and down in anticipation. I probably clapped my hands with glee, too. At the last minute, it was decided to use a straight actor instead.

The company apologized for my inconvenience by sending me a crate of champagne — which was pinched before it got to me!)

When Ford wanted to use an English actor to promote their new car, in 1979, they did a tremendous amount of market research to choose the right person. They hosted parties all over America to which they invited prospective customers and a questionnaire was passed around. People had to choose, from a number of well-known British actors, who they would actually prefer to sell them their new Ford: the person they considered the most English, the most friendly and the most pleasant. Guess who was chosen?

Yes, clever old me, bounder, cad, absolute rotter that I was! I won hands down over Sir Ralph Richardson, Wilfrid Hyde White, Robert Morley and a couple of others. Ford sent a publicity woman from the States to my home in Spain to offer me the job. I got £5,000 a day for that one and it took about six days to make.

I was filmed beside the *Queen Mary* at Long Beach and in front of London Bridge in Arizona. I had to lament something like this: 'You Yankee chaps have stolen the dear old *Queen Mary* and London Bridge. Now you've taken our quiet. The new Ford has been tested against the Rolls-Royce and it turns out it is just as quiet.' I gave a fulsome leer and concluded, 'I don't mind personally, but the *Queen* is hopping mad.'

I did ads for Fruit of the Loon for a long period. Among other things, I was seen on water-skis, struggling in a quicksand and tied to an old-fashioned train. It was a beautifully shot series.

Another series that went on and on was for vermouth. From time to time I had to fly out to Italy for a couple of weeks' work, always in different locations. Eventually, we covered the whole of the country. Now that *was* an arduous assignment. I had to be ready to begin at dawn, so it meant rising at six a.m. The Italians, more than other nationalities, never seemed satisfied and their commercials were also much longer. They took shot after shot. They drove themselves potty – and everyone else.

The theme of the series was that I was supposed to be following somebody who was never seen. It was just an excuse to show me and vermouth in beauty-spot settings. Once, I was photographed elegantly garbed, leading a cow in the middle of Rome, near the Spanish Steps. Another time, in one of those historic old Tuscany towns, I was filmed sitting at a table, on top of a car, dressed in black coat, striped trousers and bowler hat enjoying a cup of tea poured from a silver teapot. (Why I was drinking tea to advertise vermouth is quite a point!)

Unlike Mars bars, I didn't spit the vermouth out. So by the end of a day's shooting, taking into account all those retakes ... well, imagine!

Some hilarious things happened. When we filmed in Turin, I phoned a friend in a nearby town but was cut off at the start of the conversation. I explained to the operator that I had heard my friend but the moment I started to speak, the hotel cut him off. Ten minutes later, my phone rang and the operator said, 'Signor, I cannot find any trace of the Hotel Cutimoff.'

Each commercial I regarded like a film part. It had a story-line and planned camera angles, just as when making a film.

Very often I didn't like the product I was advertising, but that did not make the way I played my part any the less convincing. There was nothing in the contract to say that I had to *like* the product.

It would be impossible to compile a list of all the commercials I appeared in. There were so many. Van Heusen shirts with Diana Dors in the early days of fame ... shaving soap in Italy ... Gordon's Gin with a script that I had to learn in five languages ... an American soft drink ... gas stoves with Mike Bentine as co-chef...

One of the most famous I ever made was for Benson and Hedges. It won a world prize. You probably remember it. Eric Sykes and I were in a cellar blasting our way through a safe. Sykes put his hand through the hole and strained his arm as far as it would go to see what he could find – nothing!

Then I stepped forward and reached into the hole. That's when the camera cut to another shot. My hand was seen groping about the inside of a cigarette-vending machine in a London underground station. It was tough work – those things always were – but right from the beginning I sensed that it was going to be a classic.

Benson and Hedges were keen to continue the combination of Sykes and me in their ads, but Eric cried off. He told the booking agency he didn't want to be Terry-Thomas's stooge any more. He had played my man in *Those Magnificent Men in Their Flying Machines* and in *Monte Carlo or Bust*. I suppose he thought he might get type-cast if we had gone on with the fags sequence.

Eric didn't say anything to me and I must admit I was a bit surprised when I heard. We had always got on so well. I'd been to his house. We had dined out together. Everyone thought, quite rightly, that we were the greatest of pals. I regarded him as a clever performer who always made a lot more out of his character (however small the part) than was written in the script. It would have been nice to go on doing commercials with him and I was sorry that Eric felt like that about it.

For some time I had toyed with the idea of buying a country home but my search in leafy villages for a suitable place in the Home Counties had been in vain. Just as well. After a few years of Californian sunshine, I began seriously to think of moving out of Britain permanently and settling in a warmer clime. I was doing more and more in America (yet I didn't fancy moving *there* for good) and less and less work (because I chose it that way) in Britain.

Although I loved London, and always will (except Finchley) I couldn't stand the weather. Some people seemed to thrive on the tough climate, but not I. I have always been a bronchial person and used to keep myself fit by hunting during the winter. But as soon as I could no longer spare the time to hunt, I suffered. I became the typical Englishman with his usual bloody cold. I really couldn't see the point of working sixteen hours a day to keep myself in throat pastilles. And those heating bills were just astronomical.

So Belinda and I started house-hunting. We both had a feeling that somewhere abroad there was a place made for us. But where? To find it, we travelled extensively – just took off for a few days, between films, to various points of the globe. We considered everywhere from Honolulu to Australia and back again.

I visited dozens of islands because the idea of an island-home appealed to me. But I was never able to find one where I was completely happy. Each idyllic-seeming paradise would turn out to be too hot, too humid, too inaccessible for easy commuting, too Americanized for my liking or just not suitable full stop.

I decided to try Ibiza because of a coincidence. In Bel Air one morning, when the mail arrived, I had a letter from an artist friend in London telling me that a picture I'd ordered was ready. There was a P.S: 'How about buying a super little cottage overlooking the loveliest bay in Ibiza for somewhere to hang it?'

At that moment a man walked across the patio below me whom I didn't recognize. I shouted, 'What are you doing down there?' When the man turned I saw that it was Denholm Elliott. He joined me on the balcony and over a bottle of champagne he told me that he had just finished building a house. *In Ibiza.*

The coincidence was too much for me. There and then I decided to go back to the rocky, sun-drenched island in the Mediterranean, to see if that was the place I had been seeking, though I doubted if it were. The only time I had visited the Balearic island, I had not been smitten by it at all. I was only there for a few hours en route by ferry from Majorca to the mainland. My first impression when I had got off the boat for a quick walk-around Ibiza town was, true, there were lots of pretty girls about, but the streets stank. Owing to that bad-drains stench I had hated it, actually, and couldn't wait to get back on the boat.

Ibiza has always been the favourite spot of way-out drop-out people who set fashions – whether called Bohemians, beatniks or hippies. At that particular time they were beatniks. I remember that the girls were all dressed in a Chelsea-spiv sort of way in tatty Bohemian clothes, the style of that time. They had hand-woven baskets slung over their shoulders with an Ibizenco hound sitting in the basket. They all had long, lank hair and round their ankles were tied coloured scarves to show – it was explained to me – that they were 'engaged'. No wonder Ibiza had seemed to be a dreadfully smelly place full of contrived people.

However. Almost immediately after the chat with Denholm, Belinda and I aimed for Ibiza en route to Monaco where I was to do a TV special which would be presented by Princess Grace. We found plenty of property available on the island and Belinda and I did some enjoyable house-hunting on horseback. This time I was mad about the sparkling Spanish island with its whitewashed houses and turquoise sea. We had to break off looking at villas and go to Monte Carlo to film the programme.

In March 1956, the BBC had cancelled a sketch I had written called 'Heirs and Graces' for my TV show, *Strictly T-T*. I was to have impersonated Prince Rainier of Monaco and Lorrae Desmond was to have played Grace Kelly. I did not think the sketch was in bad taste, but Auntie Beeb did. So I hurriedly had to write new material.

Perhaps Princess Grace never knew about that. She certainly didn't mention it when we met for the first time on location for that TV spectacular near her palace home.

I was surprised that she was so soft-spoken that one could hardly hear her. She was completely professional but off the set she was exclusive and kept herself apart from the crew. I think she was inherently regal and placid.

I remember how she started off the show: 'This is my home, Monte Carlo. People come here from all over the world. Some by road. Some by rail. Some by plane. Some by water...'

This part of the dialogue coincided with my appearing in black jacket, striped trousers and bowler hat. Then they altered the lens and it was revealed that I was on water-skis. Of course, I sang 'The Man Who Broke the Bank at Monte Carlo'.

Later in the 60-minute programme, I had the truly breathtaking experience of driving a Formula 1 over the Monte Carlo circuit while Gilbert Becaud, driving an ordinary racing car, sang to me as we whistled round the corners.

I found I would have a few days to spare before the shooting of my final scene. So Belinda and I returned to Ibiza to continue our search for a home.

We had hardly arrived when the TV company wanted to contact me urgently. As they had no idea where I was staying they sent a cable to every hotel and pension on the island. They wanted to make sure they'd find me, and it worked. Whenever Belinda and I passed a hotel, hall porters and pageboys rushed out shouting and waving telegrams.

We decided that yes, Ibiza was the place where we wanted to make our home. But we could not find a 'desirable villa' to suit us.

Quite apart from a perfect house we needed a good access road. Mains water. Electricity. Telephone. A wonderful view was essential. Difficult to find all those features in one job lot in Ibiza which was then still fairly primitive.

When nothing ready-made turned up, our thoughts turned to buying land and building on it to our own stipulations. But by now I had become a bit of a tourist attraction. The locals smelt riches. I was offered a pleasant plot of land for £32,000. The price was too steep and I turned it down. Later, it was sold to someone else for £8,000.

The day I bought a plot of land was the very day I met The Man Who Knew Terry-Thomas. I popped into a bar for a drink and a chap assured me that current rumours going round that Terry-Thomas was property-hunting on the island were unfounded. For some reason he didn't recognize me. I was very tanned and wearing a knitted Moorish hat to keep the sun off.

'How do you know Terry-Thomas isn't here buying land?' I said, in a disguised voice.

'Oh, Terry's a good friend of mine,' replied this chap who I had never seen in my life. 'He'd have contacted me if he'd been here. I know for a fact that he's not going to buy anything.'

'Tell me,' I asked. 'I've often wondered … what's Terry-Thomas really like?'

And the chap said, 'Contrary to what people think, Terry-Thomas is actually frightfully modest; not at all conceited.'

Modest? Me? I didn't bother to listen to him any longer.

What we ended up with after all our searching, was half a hillside at San Carlos, 600 feet above sea-level at its lowest point. It had only one of our original requirements: the view. It was the superb panorama across pine, olive, fig, carob and almond trees to a distant bay that decided us. Straight ahead one saw the sea and over one's left shoulder was the sea again. It was the most beautiful setting imaginable.

But there were no 'mod cons' at all and it was practically cut off from any form of communication – an access road would have to be excavated. The tumbledown farmhouse that went with the land was very run down. A hill-fire had devastated the undergrowth leaving charred roots, blackened stumps and a few stunted firs. I was so keen to see something growing on that lifeless bit of land that I started by putting a few weeds in.

As I have always been allergic to architects, I decided to do the house myself. I realized it would mean being on hand as much as possible to supervise the workmen. Film commitments already planned would also mean I would have to commute between Ibiza and Hollywood, Ibiza and Rome and Ibiza and Paris. It would be tough going with all that dodging about but I had never shirked hard work.

As my operational base for the next year – the time I

reckoned it would take to complete the house – I rented
Viscount Maugham's villa perched on a delightful bit of
rocky coastline. It was very showy, all white walls and a
Gainsborough hanging over the fireplace. Festoons of
bougainvillea climbed the outside walls and practically
smothered the place – beautiful.

The only dull note was the kitchen. It was a rotten
kitchen, but, nevertheless, some pretty good meals were
produced in it by a succession of cooks. I felt the villa was a
suitably happy place to leave Belinda and Tiger while I
dashed off to earn a few more thousands towards the cost of
our 'dream-house'.

The Spanish laws are stricter now, but in those days it was
possible to build virtually anything in Ibiza without any
official plans being drawn up. A bit of money would change
hands to pave the way, or one might need only to be well in
with the mayor's cousin's maid's brother, to be able to go
ahead and build what one wanted without having to go
through that annoying rigmarole of getting plans passed.

I found a local firm of builders and explained the house I
had in mind, which was to be built around the existing
farmhouse. The men clamoured to get started but having no
plans, and knowing I'd often have to be away and unable to
instruct them, I could see many obstacles arising. So Belinda
and I moulded the shape of our dream-house out of a big
lump of flour-and-water dough. It is wonderful model-
making material, dough. One can do anything with it. The
builder referred to this very detailed, bread maquette all the
way through.

Belinda, meanwhile, made a scrapbook of ideas and
thoughts as they came to us so that nothing would be
overlooked. Materials to be used, effects to be achieved,
features not to be forgotten, colours – anything, in fact, that
was relevant, was recorded for reference in the book.

I measured the house on the ground. I paced it out, using
a method whereby, as I was to find out to my cost, one was
likely to come a cropper!

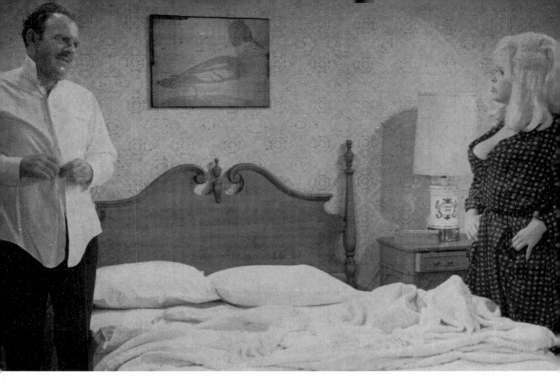

With two leading ladies. *Top* Jayne Mansfield in *A Guide for the Married Man* (1967). *Bottom:* Doris Day in *Where Were You When the Lights Went Out?* (1968). (*Cinema Bookshop*)

'Woof woof' — my dog impression. (*Terry Daum*)

No one ever accused T-T of
keeping his feet firmly on
the ground! (*Terry Daum*)

Supervising progress on my
'dream house' in Ibiza,
Summer 1967. (*Terry Daum*)

My shirt and matching Mercedes Benz were multi-coloured!
(*Terry Daum*)

Dining out at Mario's in Majorca, while on a weekend visit to Pat, with Tiger, aged 10. Chef Mario (seen cuddling my ex-wife) still owns the restaurant in El Terreno, in partnership with my old mate, Frankie Vaughan.

Tea for two T's. Tastefully togged in a tailored tapestry jacket,
a tremendously tanned T-T taking tea on a terrace in Ibiza.
(*Terry Daum*)

With just a few lines as a guide, rooms looked much smaller than they were. One then tended to exaggerate and the rooms turned out larger than they were ever intended to be.

The pleasant thing of directing operations oneself and not having an architect was that mistakes could be rectified as one went along. When the proportion of a doorway or window was not to my liking, I had a bit hacked off or added another course of stone. When I wanted another staircase put in, we just got on with it. Nothing was irredeemable.

With a separate guest-house nearby, we worked out we would have about thirty rooms, including five kitchens. When they wrote about the house, the Press always picked on the abundance of kitchens as a jokey item. But to me those functional kitchens made good sense. Two of them were situated on opposite sides of the ground floor. One was in the guest-house. One upstairs in the nursery. And the remaining one was attached to my bathroom/bedroom/dressing-room complex which would be completely shut off from the rest of the house. Oh yes, kitchens were very useful things to have about the place.

To find the local red stone for the two-bedroomed guest-house, I drove round the island carrying a hammer. I knocked off bits of rock and had them test-surfaced until I found the right stuff. I didn't want the house to stand out as being obviously new. The mellowed red stone enabled it to nestle unobtrusively in the pines as though it had been there for years.

A small army of workmen moved in and soon one could see what the house was going to be like, provided one kept a beady eye on the builders. I had to be around them to get things done because they did very little when I wasn't there. It was terribly infuriating. It didn't make sense to me why people did not do the job they were paid to do, but that, I have since found out, is the nature of the Ibizencos. It meant that whenever I had to be away from the island, little progress was made on the house. I didn't let this affect my work. I just accepted that when I got home I would have to get the whip out again.

Belinda was unable to help because she had been forced to take to her bed. She was pregnant for the second time. In view of the complications she had experienced with Tiger, the doctor thought it sensible that she should rest for six months. I took Polaroid pictures as the house took shape to keep Belinda up to date with developments. I also carried a walkie-talkie radio whenever I was on the site so that Belinda could call me if she needed to.

What with another baby on the way, a dream-house going up, a swimming pool being dug out and a tennis court and landscaped garden being laid out, it was a very productive time for us.

To unwind and get away from the dust and noise of the cement mixers and drills for a bit, I sometimes took myself off for a spot of water-skiing, which I found most relaxing. One day I took a tumble when the wrong wave came up which aggravated some trouble caused a couple of years earlier when Belinda and I had been in Acapulco.

The man who had been steering the speed-boat there, when I water-skied, had had no idea of what he was doing. He was dangerous, in fact. He caused me to crash rather badly and I did the splits, which did all sorts of unspeakable damage.

That accident had put me out of action, both workwise and 'horizontally' for some weeks. (By 'horizontally' I mean, in my coy way, that until the problem had cleared up, Belinda and I had only been able to wave to each other across our huge double bed!) Now here I was, in the wars again in that same delicate area of my body.

The house progressed but I became a little worried about Belinda's health. She was very depressed and had seemed to have lost interest in everything – even the house – since being confined to her bed. The island was then alive with hippies wearing weird and wonderful clothes and all madly into flower power. I expect Belinda felt she was missing out on a few 'happenings' by having been banished to bed.

To cheer her up, I had my cream Mercedes Benz painted over with hundreds of minuscule terracotta, green, brown and yellow flowers to match my favourite Liberty print shirt. It took two people a month to paint, by which time they were both cross-eyed. At least it got Belinda out of bed, briefly, to gape at the car, and she gave a small giggle. But I was still concerned about her.

So I got in touch with George Pinker, then the Royal family's gynaecologist (and President of the Royal College of Obstetricians and Gynaecologists) and asked him if he would come to Ibiza and take a look at her.

We had a jolly time on the night of his arrival and next morning I took him to the rocks at the bottom of the garden for a swim in the sea. After breakfast, George put on his Harley Street suit, got out his notebook and was ushered into Belinda's bedroom.

She was looking very regal, propped up in Robin Maugham's bed which was decorated with his coat of arms, in blue and gold.

George had nearly finished his examination when our local GP, Dr Comacho, arrived and joined in the fun. But Belinda was getting tired of being the centre of attention by this time. She suddenly said, very sweetly in Spanish, 'Enough of this. I want to talk to you, Dr Comacho, about my husband's *cojones*.'

The doctor's reaction was dramatic. 'No. No! *NO!! Testiculos!*' he said.

He turned his back on her to hide his face and burst into uncontrollable laughter. What Belinda had said, in her clear, soft-toned way, was the equivalent of a duchess saying: 'I want to chat about my husband's bollocks!'

To pacify her, Dr Comacho – wiping away tears of laughter from his face – took me into a broom cupboard off Robin's bedroom and examined me for any injury resulting from my latest water-ski crash.

By late summer, 1968, the house was ready. Taking into account the £10,000 it had cost to rectify a few mistakes, the whole thing came to about £100,000. I was well-pleased. We had created not merely a dream-house, according to the locals, but a dream-*palace*.

At the end of August, our second son came along.

I searched my head for an original name and came up with Trumper, which my dictionary informed me meant a splendid person. I had thought of calling the baby Zenda, as in 'The Prisoner of' because I had so enjoyed the film (the first version). But I decided that Trumper would be more suitable.

This unusual name did not please one person who found it, for some unexplained reason, offensive. In *The Sun*, a gentleman called the Reverend Arthur Alistair Malcolm Sandemann, vicar of Cressing in Essex, accused Belinda and me of preposterous and ridiculous behaviour in naming our son Trumper.

From Rome, where I was making a film, I wrote a letter of defence to *The Sun*. '…Although the vicar's reaction was predictable, I feel that I owe it to my family that etymologically and euphonically, there is nothing even slightly preposterous or ridiculous about this name. According to the Oxford dictionary, a "trump" is "a courageous person of exceptional generosity; an excellent fellow." As for the sound of the name, this is a matter of taste. 'Chacun à son goût', which loosely means, 'You've either got taste, or you haven't.'

'The Vicar of Cressing need not be depressing about our son being laughed at and mocked, because he will not be exposed to that sort of person, unless by some strange chance he goes to Cressing. Trumper has borne the name for two weeks now and seems to be bearing up very well under it. But if, at some time, he decides he does not like his name, we hope that he will have the guts and imagination of another excellent fellow who, objecting to his name, Nigel Davies, rechristened himself: Justin de Villeneuve.'

Tiger, then four-and-a-half, had the final say on the subject. When he first saw the robust new baby nestling in

Belinda's arms, Tiger said, 'He's not like a baby, he's just like a cushion!'

Trumper has been known as that ever since. Except that we spell it Cushan, as in the place where they made those famous carpets in what was once Armenia and is now Turkey.

My younger son introduces himself to everyone as Cushan and says he has no intention of ever being known as anything else.

8   Party Talk ... and Perfectionism

My idea of throwing a party was that it should be exclusive. I soon learned that in Ibiza people wouldn't accept that. There were many who would make it their business to find out, 'Where is tonight's party?' and just arrive. So we always had at least half a dozen uninvited guests. I never liked to invite more than thirty guests at a time, but often there were far more people milling around than that.

I had a lot of ding-dongs because I didn't hesitate if I saw intruders about to scoff my chicken, paella or apple crumble. I marched up to them, asked who they were, why they were there and then ordered them out. They always protested, of course, that somebody or other had invited them to come.

On one occasion a black man I had never seen before, loomed out of the darkness and said, 'Where's the bar?' I said, 'Over there.' And he went straight off to a 20-foot drop. I never found out whether he survived. At another of our parties, three dozen gate-crashers arrived together and immediately ate all of Belinda's food (carefully catered for the twenty-odd people who had been invited). We met a trio of musicians somewhere who were so good we invited them to come along for our next party. By the time they arrived, the trio had developed into a fifteen-strong band and brought about twenty-five hangers-on with them – to turn the pages of their music, I supposed. That time there was nothing I could do about it. I just had to grit my gap and put up with them.

To gate-crashers I was mean. To my guests, I tried to be as accommodating as possible.

Swiss artist Edith Irving, who's been an island resident for years, swears she saw me energetically chasing a pretty girl through one of my parties, naked. I honestly don't remember being naked, but it's likely. If Edith says so ... I'm sure she's a very truthful lady.

Edith's ex-husband, Clifford Irving, was once a frequent topic of conversation. He was handsome, a great womanizer, and got a mention on the sun-kissed café terraces every other day after his controversial biography of billionaire recluse, Howard Hughes, was proved to be a fake.

Long before that scandal broke, I'd met Clifford at Madrid airport looking a bit uncertain as to where to get his ticket for Ibiza. We were both going home for Christmas. I showed him the right counter and he parked his Ibizencan shoulder-basket on me to look after.

'Keep an eye on it, Terry. That's Howard Hughes's life-story,' he said, pointing to the thick MS on top of the basket.

I thought he was pulling my leg. If I'd known what a furore that book was going to cause, I'd have had a quick gander.

Earlier, Clifford had written a book about another island resident, Elmyr de Hory, a gentle, dry-humoured Hungarian who had fooled the art world for years with his fine, fake paintings.

I couldn't believe it when Elmyr was exposed. Only a short time before, I had gone to his oddly situated cliffside house to ask him some technical tips about building swimming pools. And I had been horrified at the very, *very* ugly pictures – his own work – which were hanging on his walls.

It turned out he had this incredible talent for being able to paint imperceptibly in the style of several 'masters'. But the talent went slightly askew when he painted as himself. Original 'Elmyrs' were awful! But he once did a copy of a Dufy picture – a girl on a horse – for Robin Maugham, which I coveted and would certainly have bought like a shot if I'd been given the chance.

Robin Maugham was a most disciplined writer. He used to work steadily at a desk on his roof, every afternoon until three. Then he'd have a very drinky lunch with just three or four guests. He usually served good Ibizencan food and always excellent wine. None of those Hollywood-style quarter bottles for Robin. Actually, as he was diabetic, he drank far more than was good for him.

Though he was a good friend of mine and I loyally read his works, I found all his books – with the exception of *Somerset and All the Maughams* and *The Link* – rather dreary.

The kaleidoscope of well-known residents and famous visitors to Ibiza was as colourful, in its way, as anything in Hollywood. Everybody congregated at Sandy's Bar, in Santa Eulalia del Rio. Irishman Sandy Pratt had opened it in 1958 before the Balearic tourist boom began. En route to Majorca from the mainland, Sandy, fresh from reading law at Trinity, did the inevitable two-hour stopover in Ibiza and fell in love with the place. He never reached Majorca. For 700 pesetas a month, he rented a house with no water, no light and no windows and spent £600 turning the ground floor into a bar that was described in subsequent guide-books to the island as 'an absolute must'.

Quiet-talking Sandy, not noticeably an extrovert, never envisaged his modest bar making such an international impact.

He still cannot explain why it did, except that for some years it was the only 'foreign bar' and had the only available telephone which all and sundry used when they had to ring anywhere in the world or leave a number where they could be reached. He also encouraged the bar to become a *poste restante* so that instead of having letters delivered to their outlying villas, all the foreign residents – including me – had their mail addressed to the bar.

Sandy's thus became a gathering place with everyone indulging in at least one of Sandy's succulently mixed Bloody Marys or *hierbas* (the local liqueur) at midday, as they sorted through their mail. I used to walk five kilometres a day to collect my letters, have a chatty drink and see who was around. It was a ritual I very rarely missed.

Sandy always turned up when invited to parties. It was quite a puzzle how he managed it because he went to several parties every day. He made a quick appearance, then left. I regarded him as one of the family. Everybody, in fact, liked to regard themselves as a friend of his.

He was always on hand, between shaking cocktails, to act as honorary lawyer-cum-general-adviser to newcomers who were about to buy property and were faced with the inevitable tangles of red tape. If anyone was in trouble, they went without hesitation to Sandy who had a magical way of clearing up problems.

He has now given up his bar and taken up landscape gardening on the island, so these days when we meet, we gossip about plants instead of people.

Columnists from the popular dailies, like the *Daily Mail*'s Charles Greville, used to come to Ibiza for the weekend and compose their Monday page with quotes from Sandy's customers and their house-guests, all 'diary in-names' that could be picked out in black type. Among those who had houses in the area were: Diana Rigg, Nina and Frederick, Nigel Davenport and Maria Aitken (when they were married), Jon Pertwee, Richard Todd and Denholm Elliott.

Denholm now travels extensively, spends a lot of time in the East, buys houses and makes films the year round. He is rarely in Ibiza these days. He and his lively wife, Susie, used to have some colourful gatherings. I once saw a most striking-looking nun downing a pint of beer on the roof of Denholm's house. She wore a thick, coarsely grained robe and had a silver crucifix hanging down to her waist. What struck me most about her were her hands: large, well-formed, long-fingered, substantial hands.

'Who's the nun?' I asked Denholm.

And he said, 'That's no nun. That's April Ashley.'

April, the famous sex-change model who married Lord Rowallan's son, was in Ibiza for a season. Wearing off-the-shoulder gowns, she used to act as hostess at bachelor Robin Maugham's dinner parties. That summer April had the distinction of owning the deepest voice on the island. She came out with some very droll sayings and we had several giggles together.

It hardly ever rained in Ibiza. I adored the relentless sun, but it did not suit all visitors, actor Ronnie Fraser for one. He wore a tight bowler-hat all the time he was on the island and sweated like a haggis.

I used to see a bowler coming along towards me, realize that a flushed, rather damp Ronnie would be underneath it ... and run.

The Hon Michael Campbell, brother and heir of Lord Glenavy (the late Patrick Campbell) certainly enjoyed his stay in Ibiza. I never saw him other than that he was merry. On the day he was leaving, he said to me as I was sitting in my car, 'I shan't see you again, Terry, I'm going back to Dublin. So give me a Parthian Shot.'

He didn't say – as most people would – 'parting shot'. He was very careful about that sort of thing, he liked it to be known that he knew a thing or two about the classics.

So I started the engine and said to Michael, 'Well, cheerio ... PATRICK'. And drove off with a roar.

Sir Laurence Olivier and Joan Plowright came to spend the day with us while they were renting a financier's house nearby. Despite having got over some form of operation, Sir Laurence (as he still was, then) was in fine form.

'Do you still drink?' I asked him.

'Rather,' he said. 'Why?'

'Well,' I said, 'I thought perhaps with all those operations you've had, you might have had to scrub round it.'

'Oh no, dear fellow, no,' he said. And I noticed that he

joined everybody else, measure for measure.

He spent most of the time mastering an Italian hunting horn I had. Eventually he played it quite well.

Then we had a sing-song. Joan Plowright, wearing a pretty yellow hat, thumped out 'April Showers' on the piano. Larry accompanied her on the horn and Belinda and I exuberantly bellowed the words.

During lunch I mentioned that I had recently seen my neighbour, Diana Rigg, in *Abélard and Héloïse*, a play which I had felt compelled to sit through because I had not had the guts to walk out.

'Well, I'd have walked out if I were bored,' said the future First Lord of the Stage.

'What excuse would you have given?' I asked.

'Oh simple! I'd just have said that it wasn't my sort of theatre,' he replied.

Abélard and Héloïse was the play in which Diana Rigg had a much-publicized, albeit brief, nude scene. Frankly, I'd missed it because I was looking at another part of the set at that moment. In any case, I wouldn't have discovered anything new about Diana. Every day when I walked to San Carlos, our nearest village, I had to pass sun-lover Diana's garden and she rarely bothered to put anything on for my benefit.

Ursula Andress was another who had property on Ibiza and I'd often see her around with Jean-Paul Belmondo, who was her escort for a time. Ursula stopped coming to the island after the house she had commissioned to be built for her developed some dangerous cracks in the walls and started slipping into the sea.

Lionel Bart's stay in Santa Eulalia ended dramatically with his being escorted back to Britain by a Red Cross nurse.

Lionel, and a close friend of his called Glenn, rented Denholm Elliott's house and all was fine until Glenn got too friendly with Elinore, the girl helping in the house. This state of affairs so upset Lionel that he started drinking to put it out of his mind. He consumed so much alcohol that his stomach was aggravated and he haemorrhaged in the middle of the night. His teeth fell out in the spurt of blood.

For some reason, Belinda was called in to help nurse him and she reported that Lionel kept up a jolly line in jokes against himself while spitting blood everywhere.

All this was very unpleasant for him, so he was taken to a clinic in Ibiza. He discharged himself after three days and stayed in our house until the Red Cross nurse he'd sent for arrived to take him home.

As for Glenn and Elinore, the last I heard, they were happily shacked up together in Ireland.

The only time I took part in a circus – apart from a TV 'special' presented as a circus – was in Ibiza. An impoverished Spanish circus company was down on its luck. The twenty-strong company had not made enough money, during its short season in Santa Eulalia, to cover expenses back to the mainland. I was persuaded by a friend of mine to help out at a specially arranged performance.

From the local residents were mustered volunteer instrumentalists, dancers and singers. Some really beautiful clothes were run up to ensure that the evening went well.

I did an impromptu act with my sons' toy gramophone. Nigel Davenport mucked in as ring-master, or rather ring-mistress.

He got hold of some women's clothes (which made him look grotesque) and nearly killed himself wearing his sister's shoes. It was a great night and the Cirque Bleu company made enough money to get home.

For the first few years, Ibiza really was the unblemished paradise that I'd envisaged: a beautiful island, restful if one sought peace and unbelievably lively if one didn't. The sun shone constantly (with care one could keep a year-round tan) and even in winter, except for one or two days, the sea was a shimmering and inviting blue.

All my life I had suffered from bronchial trouble which had caused me thousands of sleepless, sweat-soaked nights with stomach-churning coughing attacks and a general feeling of doom. Once I was in Ibiza I was free of it. Once I got settled in my house, 600 ft up, the condition seemed to leave me and I began sleeping like a baby.

Dr Comacho, the local GP, told me that if anybody came to him with bronchitis he asked them where they lived. If they said they lived by the sea he advised them to move to the mountains, and if they lived in the mountains he told them to move to the sea.

All over the island one saw grubby hippies wearing bright clothes adorned with tiny mirrors, beads, bells and flowing, batik-printed chiffon scarves. They all smiled benignly as they gathered flowers from the roadside to decorate themselves and stick in their hair.

There was a blissful, exultant aura about Ibiza and every time I flew home from making some film or commercial, I felt content to be back. Life was good. I was successful and rich. I had a fine family and a magnificent house.

It all seemed too good to last. And it didn't last. Perverse, petulant Parkinson's Disease was waiting to pounce and take me over so that my life-style would never be the same again, knocking my obsessive perfectionistic tendencies for six.

I wasn't a perfectionist at school. It came on when I seriously took up the stage as a career, and it quickly encroached on my private life. Eventually, perfectionism took me over completely which, I admit, didn't make it easy for the people who had to live and work with me.

It has calmed down a bit in the last few years. For instance, I no longer change my underwear two or three times a day as I used to, but it's still there, this need that everything should always be just right. Sometimes it depresses me enormously to have set myself such a high standard. It really tumbles my spirits when I recognize that I'm doing things which are unnecessarily ambitious.

I remember doing a charity show for a man who said, 'Thank you Terry. I'm most grateful. Now here's a nice drink.'

And I said, 'It isn't a nice drink, nowhere near. The gin is a doubtful brand. The tonic is with sugar. There's no lemon and no ice. Apart from that it's in a cheap glass and what's more the glass is dirty.'

There was little reaction from my host. He just mumbled something unintelligible.

Muck, dust, grease and unpleasant smells all worry me to a point of distraction. When I've met dirty people it's affected me terribly. I always keep two pairs of bedroom slippers in use. And I change them every two hours or so. The ones I've taken off are popped outside to air so that they won't get that 'old dog' smell.

I can't put up with stuffy rooms and I abhor cigarette smoke.

It was only his smoking habits that brought Buster Keaton down, in my estimation. Otherwise I picked up such a lot from this charming man. In *It's a Mad Mad Mad Mad World* we went out to his house to shoot one scene and I admired his ability to make everything he did appear exciting. He had to push a motor car and though you wouldn't imagine there could be much business to make out of pushing a car, Buster was able to build it into a special thing. Instead of going straight to the car, as everybody else would, he first summed it up thoughtfully and then moved in to push it. I found all his actions pretty to watch – except smoking. He was a chain smoker and there wasn't anything pretty about that. Then he became just like any other person puffing away at a fag.

While on the subject of smoking ... I noticed that Sharon Tate, who was pregnant when we made *Seven Times Seven*, used to hold her cigarettes in a most furtive way.

When I asked why, she whispered, 'My husband might be hiding and watching. He doesn't like me to smoke because of the baby.'

We were shooting in a field and I pointed out that there was no place in sight where Roman Polanski could possibly have been hiding, except up a nearby tree.

Sharon replied, 'He climbs trees very well.'

Going back to my perfectionism, stains on summer-weight

suits or suede shoes would come pretty close to displeasing me more than anything else in the world. And I expect table and bed linen to be spotless at all times. Grace Kelly had the right idea. Her bed-linen used to be changed daily, twice if she took an afternoon siesta and rumpled the sheets.

I don't think many people are serious enough about food and presentation. They pretend to be, but they're not. As a perfectionist, I demand hot food served on hot plates and always accompanied by sparkling table napkins and crisp, hot toast. I don't mind eating off a tray if the tray is perfectly laid and presented.

I realize all this might seem unnecessarily finicky to people who don't care about the finer points of eating and drinking.

(This reminds me of a regimental sergeant-major who took his wife to the Savoy on her birthday. 'Oh no, not the Savoy,' she said.

And he said, 'Yes. The Savoy. And you're going to enjoy it whether you like it or not.'

They ordered asparagus and finger bowls were brought. He asked, 'What's this?' And she said, 'Does it matter?'

'It certainly does,' he said. 'Waiter! What are these bowls for?'

And the waiter said, 'It is possible, sir, that you will get some butter sauce on your fingers. These bowls are for washing your fingers.'

And the wife said, 'There you are y'see. Silly questions get silly answers.')

I hate shoddy service. When I get good service I acknowledge it. I used to hunt near Taunton and have a meal on the train on the way back to London. My experience on one journey, in November 1956, prompted me to send this letter to the *Daily Express*.

'Sir, I recently travelled on the 6.25 train from Taunton to London and enjoyed a most delectable meal, beautifully served. How nice to praise rather than blame. But stay. If these chaps can do it on the 6.25 why cannot the staff on all restaurant cars? I mean – as nice as Taunton is, we can't keep going there, can we?'

I always found that in restaurants, tipping was the thing that most people were not happy about. They tended to think afterwards that if they had used their nut, they could have got away with leaving the waiter much less. Personally, I have always made a rule to leave 10 per cent and was never guilty of asking other people, 'How much should one tip, here?'

I remember an aunt of mine arriving in London at my sister's flat, with a huge number of Gladstone bags, holdalls and cases. She paid the taxi-driver his fare and then she said, grandly, 'And this ... is for you!' And she handed him a silver threepenny bit.

The only time my cool was a bit shaken at gratuity time was when I had finished my meal in a Swiss restaurant and asked for my bill which seemed to be exorbitant. 'Is service included?' I asked the waiter. And he replied, 'Service yes! But not the tip!'

It was in November 1976 that I came close to snuffing it in South Africa. According to some people, I did die!

I flew to Johannesburg to be fitted with costumes for my part in the film, *King Solomon's Treasure*. I was then to go to Swaziland where the film was being shot. But I never made Swaziland.

I was in a Johannesburg clinic with bronchial pneumonia and pleurisy, fighting for my life.

I left England with a heavy cold. During the flight I felt wonky and asked the stewardess for some aspirins. When I left the plane I staggered as though I was drunk. My theory is that the rarefied atmosphere (Johannesburg being so high up) boiled up my cold germs.

At the hotel I got the porter to send for a doctor and in the shortest space of time I had been taken to hospital on a stretcher. I felt more ghastly than I had ever felt before and I knew there was something seriously wrong with me.

I was x-rayed, my temperature was taken and various tests were made. Then, before anything else happened, I was asked for proof that I would have enough money to pay the hospital fees! News got round quickly that I was dying, or dead. The Press arrived in force, cluttering up the corridor and trying to burst into my room to snatch pictures.

Though the illness affected everything, I was aware of where I was and what was going on. I was given masses of medicaments as I struggled to hang on to life. I felt as if I were having a terrible attack of bilharziasis and the bubonic plague at the same time. For once I was stuck for a joke to ease the tension.

One of the most terrible things I had to put up with was the doctor who looked after me. At first it was obvious he'd never heard of me but he cottoned on pretty quickly when the Press started phoning him non-stop. I could hear him coming to see me when he was still miles away because he had a number of walkie-talkies strapped to his body so that his secretary, his wife, the matron, ward sisters and various nurses could all be in immediate contact with him.

What dispelled my feelings of confidence in him was the hat he hardly ever took off. It was the sort of hat you would expect to see in a fairground, a pea-green pork-pie, made of straw. I said to him with irony, 'WHAT a lovely hat, Doctor!' 'Do you like it? I'll get you one,' he said.

And I said quickly, 'Better wait and see whether I recover.'

A drowning man, it is said, sees the whole of his life parade before him. I can reveal that a dying comedian remembers all the doctor-jokes he's ever heard. I lay there for a couple of weeks feeling quite destroyed as I fought the bugs and did my damnedest to cling on. I didn't want to shut up shop. I yearned to see my family at least one more time.

Morale was not boosted when I learned that Patrick McGee had been flown from Canada to take over my rôle in the film. And all the time those bloody awful jokes raced repeatedly through my mind.

(There was this man who went to a doctor because he felt off-colour. After examining him the doctor said, 'I can't see any reason why you should feel unfit. What sort of life do you lead?'

'Oh, a very simple life,' said the chap.

'What time do you get up?' asked the doctor.

'Eight o'clock!'

'What do you do then?'

'I shave, shower and go down to breakfast.'

'What do you have for breakfast?'

'Two boiled eggs, toast, honey and tea with milk.'

'What happens then?'

'I go out to my garage and start the car up. I then go into the lavatory, vomit, come out, get in the car and drive to the office.'

The doctor inquired, 'Do you vomit every day after breakfast?'

'Of course,' said the chap, surprised. 'Doesn't everyone?'

Then there was the man who had a swollen wrist. He looked up a swollen wrist specialist in the yellow pages and went to see him.

'I have come to see you about my swollen wrist,' he said.

And the doctor said, 'Good thinking. I am a swollen wrist specialist.'

The man said, 'Yes. That's why I've come to see you.'

'Right,' said the doctor. 'I'm going to take an x-ray. When I've shown it to my partner, we'll have a little conference. I'd like you to come back tomorrow.'

The chap did.

'Ah,' said the specialist. 'You came to see me yesterday, didn't you? How's your swollen wrist?'

'I've still got it,' the man said.

'Good,' said the doctor. 'Now I have conferred with my partner and we have decided that you should bathe this wrist in hot water, as hot as you can possibly stand it. Come back next week and let me know how you got on.'

The following week, the chap returned.

'Is the wrist any better?' asked the doctor.

'No, it isn't!'

'Well, did you bathe it in hot water, as I said?'

'Yes, and all that happened was that I got a lot of blisters.'

'Go on with the treatment,' said the doctor. 'Everything will be all right.'

A week or so later the man went to see the specialist again and the doctor asked, 'How's your wrist?'

'Completely better,' said the man.

'There you are,' said the doctor. 'I told you it would be all right.'

And the man said, 'It didn't get better because of your treatment. My housekeeper noticed me bathing my wrist in hot water. She asked me what I was doing and when I told her the reason she said, "COLD water! Not hot!"

'So I swapped to cold water and it was cured immediately.'

'Cold water?' mused the doctor. 'I can't understand that. *My* housekeeper distinctly said *hot* water.')

My stay in the clinic and then in the nursing home cost a fortune because I wasn't insured. Suddenly, I looked up one day and there was Belinda with our two sons and Belinda's current au pair (or was he a boy-friend?) standing at my bedside. She had really thought I was on my last and had taken the boys out of school and flown over.

I was thrilled to see them – even the boy-friend – and their presence helped my slow recovery, even though to get them there had cost a couple of thousand quid in fares.

I foiled the undertaker and returned home with the family – and the boy-friend – drained of energy but still kicking.

It took years to get back to normal.

9   *Perfidious Parkinson's*

Comedy-writer/director, Frank Tashlin, used to trot out the following story when the conversation in Hollywood got round to fans — as it often did. Frank had gone to see John Barrymore Snr about a film they were working on. In earnest discussion, the two of them strolled up and down John's lawn in Beverly Hills. John was wearing the inevitable ivory-silk dressing-gown with coronet on the pocket and immaculate white silk scarf supporting his head.

Suddenly, a coach came down the road with a driver talking into a microphone. The peace of the afternoon was shattered by the driver's amplified nasal announcement: 'Ladies and gentlemen. We now come to the home of one of the biggest stars: The Great Profile! JESUS! There IS Mr John Barrymore himself.'

Every person in the coach pressed his face to the window for a better look and John angrily bent down to pick up a very large pebble from the base of a tree. (You have probably noticed these large stones piled around trees in hot countries. It's a good idea because it looks nice and also protects the roots from being scorched by the blazing sun.)

John hurled the pebble at the coach and bellowed at the top of his voice, 'FUCK OFF!'

Frank Tashlin said it disturbed him to think that those people in the coach, who had probably come from all parts of America, would have returned home and described this surprising incident to their friends and relatives. And everybody they told would think it was a joke. Not one single person would be believed. It was *this* fact that worried Frank.

Mr Barrymore was, perhaps, a trifle impetuous; true, some fans could be a nuisance.

When I was with Lorrae Desmond in Capri, we went to call on Gracie Fields at the world-famous swimming pool she ran there and which I found a bit over-rated.

Suddenly, Gracie was called away and a few minutes later we heard an interchange of voices and one of them got shriller and shriller. When Gracie came back, she said, 'I'm sorry about that. It was a fan from Rochdale.'

And just because that fan had travelled all the way to Capri, on holiday, she had expected to spend the whole day with Gracie Fields, chatting about Rochdale, even though she had never met the singer in her life. The shouting we'd heard was the fan turning vicious when Gracie had apologetically explained that she was occupied.

I always took fans and autograph hunters in my stride, especially when travelling by air. One was invariably going to be recognized, pointed at, approached and perhaps touched and one had to accept that it was all part of the job. It did wear rather thin, though, on one occasion.

A woman came up to me at Los Angeles airport and snapped, 'Sign this!' And she pushed a little girl forward who had an autograph book.

I had just discovered that my ticket was not in order and I would have to wait several hours for the next plane. The irritation caused by that knowledge must have shown on my face because the woman asked, 'What's the matter, Terry? Don't you like signing autographs?'

I said, 'Well, as you mention it, I might as well tell you that I don't.'

'Good God!' she said, disgustedly. 'Aren't you human?'

In October 1963, when I appeared on *The Judy Garland*

Show and sang 'Tea for Two' with her, Judy revealed herself as a fan of mine. I was really thrilled. Judy, who kept taking swigs from a bottle of Three Nuns Liebfraumilch that she dangled in her hands throughout rehearsals, came up to me and said, 'Terry-Thomas, this *is* nice! It's a real honour to have *you* on my show.'

I was so pleased that, for once, I was almost speechless. 'I … I don't know what to say,' I mumbled. And she flashed back with that dark-eyed smile: 'Just say thank-you. It is startlingly simple.'

Normally it was a matter of course to accept the big names when you worked with them, without being thrown. After all, we were all performers doing our job of work however world-famous some of us were. So when I 'guested' on TV shows with 'greats' like Sophie Tucker, Lucille Ball, Andy Williams, Perry Como, Carol Burnett, Jack Parr, Red Skelton, Tom Jones and so on, and coincided on film-sets with 'legends' such as Joan Crawford (*The Karate Killers* 1967) and Edward G Robinson (*Checkmate for McDowell*) I took it all in my stride.

But there were two exceptions who both appeared with me in *It's a Mad Mad Mad Mad World*.

I found I could not approach Spencer Tracy in a normal way or treat him like an everyday person. Despite his serious drinking problem (which did not seem to go with his personality) he was an extra-special man and it was very difficult to believe that he was real. This effect was something that emitted from him and not from other people's reaction to him.

Buster Keaton was the same. They were the only two people who ever produced in me this awe of greatness. I just couldn't meet them without being affected.

On a few occasions I've behaved like a fan myself. Antonio, the Spanish dancer, for instance, excited me more than any other artiste I'd ever seen. Many times I watched his performance and went backstage afterwards to tell him what a fantastic dancer he was. He always agreed with me!

I once sent Ann Shelton a fan-letter, a most unusual thing for me to do. When I heard her on the air singing 'Down at the Old Bull and Bush', I was so affected by her voice I felt compelled to write and congratulate her on being such a fine performer.

When Shirley Bassey made her first appearance at the Café de Paris, I was there with Sir Bernard and Lady Docker. I said to Sir Bernard, 'I don't get it. I don't think she has anything – except an appalling taste in clothes.'

He said, 'Give her a chance. She'll be very good in a year or two.'

Within less than a year Shirley had improved so much that when I heard her broadcasting from the Palladium, I phoned her immediately and congratulated her. At the end of the conversation I said, 'Well, goodnight.'

'What do you mean, goodnight?' Shirley exclaimed. 'Aren't you going to take me out to supper?'

'It's a lovely idea,' I said. 'But my girl's frightfully jealous.'

Like many artistes, Jeanne de Casalis (Mrs Feather) used to get insulting letters after her broadcasts. This worried her.

So I suggested a way how she could deal with them. Irrespective of the rude things people had written, I advised her to reply: 'Miss de Casalis thanks you for your charming letter and apologizes because her photographers have let her down. When she does have some photographs, she will be delighted to send you one.'

This always did the trick and pleased Jeanne no end.

Diana Dors probably cracked the fan-letter situation because – at least while I had intimate dealings with her – she didn't answer a single letter, complimentary or otherwise. She considered it a waste of time bothering with the silly letters she received from cranks.

I could never make up my mind whether to answer letters or not because I didn't think it would achieve much. However, when people kindly sent Christmas presents – scarves, pens, lighters, shirts – I did write, of course, to say thanks. With some of my fans, met through correspondence, I still have contact to this day.

After my near-brush with death in South Africa, I received dozens of letters from fans all over the world wishing me well. Getting that mass of mail, full of love and sympathy, touched me tremendously. It came like the applause that every performer thrives on just at the time when, laid low as I was, my ego most needed a boost.

But the letters I got then were few compared to the number I received after I appeared on television on the programme *The Human Brain* and talked frankly about the effects on me of Parkinson's Disease.

My appearance brought in £32,000 from viewers towards research in the disease.

I got hundreds of letters. Sackfuls. Some letters sympathized about the fact that I was suffering from Parkinson's, for which there was no known cure. Many were from fellow sufferers containing either words of encouragement or cries for help. Others were from fans who had enjoyed my work over the years and thought the time was right to tell me so.

This warm letter was typical. It came from a lady I'd never met, Kathleen Doig, of 27 Coleridge Road, Ashford, Middlesex.

'Dear Terry-Thomas, I was on holiday when I saw you on television, and as a fellow-sufferer of Parkinson's, I take this liberty of writing to you. Please, please, don't give in to this horrible complaint. Just fight it, as I've done. My doctor says I'm now on top of it!

'I send you my best wishes for your fight and God bless you for all the happiness you have given to the public. Hoping to see you on telly soon, yours sincerely, Kathleen Doig.'

The disease first made its presence known when I was in Australia. I had to go to a doctor about something and he asked me if I had noticed that my left hand was trembling. Actually, I hadn't. The doctor did not put forward any ideas as to what could be the reason.

Back in London, my own doctor sent me to one of the biggest names in neurology. After making tests he told me, quite calmly, that I had Parkinson's Disease and that he would prescribe drugs which I would have to take for the rest of my life. He pointed out that although drugs could control the disease, there was no curative treatment, nor any immediate prospect of a cure being found.

It was daunting news for I learned that the disease was a progressive nervous disorder that could produce (and since has) among other things: a stooped posture, shuffling gait and muscular rigidity and tremors.

I feared it would affect my job prospects so at first I tried to hide it. But when rumours of my 'drunken behaviour' on film-sets began to flourish, I admitted the real reason. It was natural that people would think I was drunk. I'd have thought the same seeing somebody behaving as I was. And as it was a condition that would get increasingly worse, I knew it would be hopeless to try to hide it. Anyway, I felt it was unfair to be labelled with having a drink problem when I didn't have one.

It wasn't long before I was incapable of acting other than very brief scenes. My left arm jerked about all over the place and this affected the rest of me and my speech.

My regular activities, pastimes and pursuits before perfidious Parkinson's intruded into my life were riding, skating, dancing, running, walking, swimming, water-skiing, reading, painting, gardening, sex-games, house-work, trampolining, playing billiards/cards/poker/table-tennis – and standing on my head.

(I was such a keen table-tennis player I used to carry a portable ping-pong table as I flitted backwards and forwards across the Atlantic. It went everywhere with me. I spent half my life playing. Mickey Rooney was a regular opponent on the set of *It's a Mad Mad Mad Mad World*. We both played to win and were evenly matched, so the games were terrific.)

Apart from walking, which I try to do every day, there's not much on that list I can still manage.

Of course I can still read, but not very well because I cannot sit for long periods or concentrate for any length of time. Writing is a chore. It's the same with billiards and those other games, including the sexy ones. After five minutes, I've had enough.

Trampolining was the best exercise I knew and I'd done it for years. I was once seen doing it on Della Reece's TV show. But jumping and landing became difficult when I became a Parkinsonian and I eventually had to give it up about five years ago. If I were foolish enough to try today I could easily be thrown off. My balance has gone hay-wire. And my strength has gone. In 1980, I also had to give up water-skiing. I had practised this exciting sport extensively for years and in Australia, so as not to waste a minute, I used to listen to test matches while water-skiing by means of having a transistor radio attached to my ear with insulating tape.

I once made enthusiastic plans to ski across the English Channel but I'm afraid that was an ambition that was never realized. Twice I attempted it. The first time I was at it for about three hours before I got bored, flagged down the speedboat when we passed the house of some friends of mine, near Dover, and popped in for a drink.

The second time was on my sixty-sixth birthday which just happened (like all my preceding birthdays and subsequent ones) to fall on Bastille Day. To raise cash for under-privileged children, I planned to ski from Littlestone in Kent to Cap Gris Nez in France – and help the French to celebrate my birthday.

But the sea conditions just weren't good enough. After a while I packed it in, did a bit of fishing, caught five mackerel and went home.

One of the most upsetting things that occurs when one suffers from Parkinson's Disease is bradykinesia – slowness of movement. How it affects me is that I have a false feeling that my foot is stuck to the ground.

It mostly comes on when I'm passing through a door but

there is never any warning when it is about to happen. An invisible wall is built up, in my mind, and my foot refuses to budge. I never know how long I am going to remain stuck like that. When I do manage to free my foot, I shamble on quickly to catch up with my brain which seems as though it has already gone ahead. Some days it's worse than others. It's infuriating. One minute I can be behaving in a perfectly normal manner; the next I have become a shaking mass of humanity.

I often think, perhaps erroneously, that being an incurable perfectionist in everything from carving to cuddling makes having Parkinson's even more of a burden to bear than to people who do not set themselves such gruelling criteria. When your whole life has been a challenge to perform all that you do perfectly, it comes hard to have to accept that from now on there are going to be no impeccable performances.

Meals are always an uncertain adventure: am I going to be able to get the food and drink to my mouth without spilling the lot over one of my lovely shirts? Telling stories has become a chore. Perhaps I can't remember a simple word, or a punch-line or even how the story goes – stories that I've known backwards for years.

(And that reminds me of the two men who were talking and one says to the other, 'I find it difficult to remember people's names.'

The other chap says, 'It's easy. You just fit their name into a pattern. For instance, if you want to remember Robert Burns, you would think of a policeman on fire – a bobbie burns, see?'

And the other says, 'Well, that isn't infallible. You might come up with Robert Browning!')

Before Parkinson's Disease took me over completely, bringing with it constant bowel trouble, intolerable gyrations and a regular attack in the afternoon which makes me immobile and for which the only cure is to lie down, I was able to do several commercials, once or twice with my left hand behind my back so that the jerking wouldn't show. One needed an understanding director, of course.

I won't say that Parkinson's Disease ever actually ruined any of my scenes. I prefer to say that some scenes had to be done more often because of my shakes.

I was once contracted to do a tea commercial at Elstree for an American company. The sponsors knew I wasn't too fit and they sent two chaps over from Chicago to supervise that the shots were what was wanted.

I'm afraid I interrupted the flow of work by not being able to perform properly. Cliff Owen, the director, wanted me to pick up a packet of tea and pop it into a teapot. I had to make several attempts before I could do it without bashing the pot all over the place.

The next morning I telephoned Cliff and said, 'Sorry about yesterday, but I do hope my wobbling arm did not hold you up too much.'

'No Terry,' he said. 'The chaps from Chicago left this morning and said they thought they had got it.'

'Good God,' I said, alarmed. 'Not Parkinson's?'

'No, the *shot!*'

For the last four years I haven't felt like accepting any work. I'm always hoping my health will improve so that I can get back into the swing of things again. I was asked to do a 'Terry-scene' with Terry Scott and Terry Wogan on television. I accepted but had to drop out because I didn't feel up to it. A pity. I'd like to work with old Terry Scott again and I'm sure I'd have enjoyed meeting that Wogan chap who comes over to me as a very worthwhile, jokey sort of card.

Deep down, I like to think it's possible that I will be able to go back to work one day. I could certainly do voice-overs without any trouble, as I did for Walt Disney's 1973 cartoon movie, *Robin Hood*.

Katharine Hepburn, a fellow-sufferer, has proved that it can be done. I saw her in a TV film in which she used her jerky arm to make the scene more dramatic. It was not obvious that she had Parkinson's Disease. It merely looked as if she were over-acting, but it came off. I think that was the first time that Parkinson's Disease had been used positively in a film.

From the gents' loo in the Beverly Hills Hotel, I once watched Kate playing tennis with great gusto.

I was rinsing my hands when Max Factor introduced himself to me. He was standing at the next sink. We exchanged pleasantries and watched with admiration, through the window, Kate doing her stuff on the court. It was clear to me that she was shaking but she coped fantastically. I was most impressed.

Largely because of being dominated by the disease, I have become more and more of a recluse. Owing to the sense of confusion it causes, I find it very difficult to behave naturally without shaking and I'm not keen to be seen like this in public, a shadow of my former self. I suppose it's my vanity that doesn't want people's image of a dashing T-T to be spoilt.

It is so easy to feel bitter and I constantly have to fight mental depression. Parkinson's would keep me in the doldrums all the time if I didn't make a perpetual conscious effort to concentrate my brain on other things. Sometimes, I'm amazed I haven't gone loopy.

I try not to dwell on the fact that my being struck by the disease prevented me from amassing another little fortune. Now that we are going through a long, protracted period of inflation, just like everyone else I can see my savings dwindling rapidly, so I could have done with another fortune.

I imagine that like me, other people (completely healthy people who don't have exorbitant medical bills) also think: 'If only I had known the price of living would get so high, I'd have been more careful in the past.'

There is no set pattern about the effects of Parkinson's Disease. It affects different people in different ways. When a doctor asked me how it affected me, I said, 'I get depressions.'

And this doctor said, 'You can't blame Parkinson's for that. You've always had depressions for obvious reasons. You have all sorts of worries and it is natural that they should depress you. You'd be depressed whether you had Parkinson's or not.'

He was probably right.

To try to buck me up, when I'm feeling low, people say, 'At least Parkinson's Disease doesn't kill.'

At the Parkinson's Disease Society, to which I have happily given support since I was first diagnosed as having the disease, they attach an enormous amount of importance to the fact that Parkinson's is not a killer. They appreciate and willingly agree that it is, or can be, painful, but stress that it doesn't actually kill.

The executive director, Tony Kilmister, has even written to the Press to say that Parkinson's should not be accused of being fatal.

I suppose I should concede that having Parkinson's is less inconvenient than say, suffering from multiple sclerosis.

When I'm feeling lousy, which is quite often, such as on the days when I have to be helped in and out of bed and need assistance to dress myself, it is easy for self-pity and melancholy brooding to take over. I wonder then why I'm being made to suffer so much. I ask myself: Where did I go wrong? Didn't I do my job properly? Surely I worked well and successfully? Was I unjust and nasty to people somewhere along the years? Is this why I am being made to pay now?

When I was in one of those despairing moods, it was even quoted in *Titbits* – and requoted in newspapers across Britain – that I had contemplated suicide. So far, quite frankly, I've never found the time!

That's got the negative side over. On the credit side, as I keep reminding myself, is the fact that I have had a full and busy life and made quite a few people laugh, which was always my intention. I've got a splendid family: a beautiful and understanding wife who has had her own problems and conquered them; a tall handsome elder son who's painting and decorating in London and a younger son, of whom I'm very proud, who is the head-boy of his school.

In self-defence I gave up drinking wine (one of the greatest pleasures of life) because it was making me feel seedy, but I still relish good food – and Belinda's a marvellous cook.

I still enjoy a good classical concert and get a special thrill when I see Spanish flamenco dancing done well.

I still get a terrific kick from smelling the fragrance of a perfect rose in a lovely garden.

I still get up early to catch the sunrise and marvel at it every time.

And I hope you'll agree, your having been kind enough to read to the end of this book, that I still have my sense of humour.

Epilogue
The Tale Behind the Tales

One sweltering afternoon in August 1983, Terry-Thomas telephoned my home in Majorca. He was ringing from the riverside house at Marlow (Bucks) which he and his second wife, Belinda, had taken for the summer to get away from the heat of Ibiza, where they lived. I had known them since their honeymoon, twenty years before, initially on a reporter/star basis. Then, over the last two decades, a good relationship had formed between us.

I usually ferried Terry from Palma airport to the little cottage at Bonanova, home of his first wife, Pat (who had once been his professional dancing partner) when he called on her for lunch. He had done this quite often until Pat's death, at eighty, earlier that year.

After his mid-morning arrival from Ibiza, I would drive him to Pat's – she was a great friend of mine – and collect him again, after tea, to take him back to the airport in time for the evening flight to Ibiza. That part of the day was when he would 'leak' a story for me to sell to a national newspaper as my 'perk' for driving him. He also spoke, off the record, about his business and marital matters.

The telephone call from Marlow on that hot afternoon, however, was more intimate and startling than our conversations had ever been before. It lasted over an hour and Terry's voice, throughout, was weak and indistinct. He was, he told me, acutely depressed. Parkinson's Disease, from which he had suffered for seven years, was affecting him more and more.

It had been two years since he had last been well enough to work and his capital was dwindling fast.

'Life is nothing for me now that I can't live as I like,' said Terry. 'One doctor said I've got about four years more to live. God forbid! I shall probably blow my brains out first. The time must come when one decides: "I'm off. I can't put up with the suffering any longer."'

(As fate turned out, the doctor was short in his estimate. Terry had six-and-a-half years still to go.)

'Some days I can't walk at all,' he went on. 'At other times, I can't speak. The perpetual shaking robs you of your dignity. You're given dope to excite you. Then more dope to calm you. No wonder your senses get muddled.

'Nobody should have to suffer like this. It's a frightening thing to say but often I think I shall have to give in. Often, it seems the only way out is suicide. The trouble is, I have two excellent teenage sons and a wife who understands me. I don't want to leave them.'

Eventually, he got round to why he was calling me. He was anxious to write the story of his life but needed help. Physically, he could no longer manage to scribble much more than his signature on a cheque.

'I've still got something useful to say before I die,' he said. 'After all, I don't feel that T-T should just limp off the stage.'

He had already tried with two co-writers to get a book together, with little success, for both attempts had quickly fallen through and advanced royalties returned to the publishers.

'Frankly, I wasn't taken by the writing of either of those two geezers,' perfectionist Terry explained. 'Just before she died, Pat suggested to me that you would be the right one to do it with me, as you know us so well. What do you think?'

I promised to go and see him when I was in England in a couple of weeks' time.

Terry audibly bucked-up at this. 'Jolly good show,' he said, briefly sounding like the T-T of old. He added, and now he was clearly joking, 'So I'll put off all thoughts of suicide until after you've been. Anyway, I can't afford to kick the bucket yet.'

Within an hour of my first visit to Marlow, in September, we started working, Terry chatting animatedly as I made notes. I returned the next morning and the next. The fourth day he felt too poorly to talk and no more work was done for nearly a week. But the notes were going well and it was obvious to both of us that we would be able to collaborate amicably. Soon, though, I would have to go back to Majorca.

'That won't stop us. This book is important to me. I'll move to Majorca,' Terry decided.

Pat had bequeathed him her quaint, yellow-shuttered cottage, S'Olivera, and in October 1983, he and Belinda arrived via Ibiza where they had put their thirty-roomed villa on the market, at £250,000.

Our sessions became a daily routine. I would arrive at eleven, Terry's best time of day, and immediately start to 'interview' him in the garden, as we sat beneath the tall palm-tree Pat had planted.

We always stopped at one o'clock by which time he would be feeling tired and ready for lunch. Even though I was co-writer at his request, he rarely volunteered information but made me work for it. He preferred to be 'brought out' by answering questions.

Terry became more and more enthusiastic as the first chapters took shape, urging me to send them immediately to a publisher. 'What's to stop us getting this book out in six weeks?' he said, gaily. I suspected that his hopes that the book would get a good Press were not so much to swell his fast-fading bank balance, which was being eaten up by expensive medical treatment, but to boost his ego. 'Yes,' he admitted, 'I'd like to be in the public eye one more time.' He planned to make promotional appearances on TV and radio, 'as long as the publisher doesn't go wild with the number'.

I had heard that co-writers had spectacular fights, but Terry and I only ever had one big difference, on a cold day when we were working indoors, which didn't please him as he was a fresh-air fiend. It was over a pithy remark that Terry claimed he had made to Danny Kaye in a hotel lift in Rome. I thought it was good, but for some reason Terry wanted to censor it.

Goading him to keep it in, I said, 'Well, if that comes out, what about the paragraph where Mickey Rooney sticks bits of carrot up his nose and smarms his hair with salad-cream? Will that be coming out, too?'

Terry jumped up in a fury and shuffled across the room with a raised fist which he brought to within one inch of my nose. 'How dare you,' he roared. 'That's the best bit in the book.'

Shaking, he retired to the bathroom for a while and I to the garden. When he joined me there, a quarter of an hour later, he said with a giggle, 'Having got that little scene over, old boy, shall we resume?'

We had no more fights. But Danny Kaye didn't make it.

As time went on I became more and more impressed by the patience and devotion shown by Belinda. I knew she had her own troubles but she always wore a gentle smile and rarely complained, though living with a progressively ailing perfectionist who had Parkinson's was no joke.

She could spend well over an hour, in the poky kitchen of the cottage, preparing a salad in the ultra-perfectionistic way that Terry expected. Above a bed of finger-torn lettuce, every twig of carrot would appear to be exactly the same size and face, say, from north to south. Symmetrical strips of cucumber, beetroot or radish, all identically chopped, would criss-cross, basket-weave fashion, from east to west. Perfect halves of scalloped boiled eggs, alternating black and green olives and apple-chunks soaked in lemon juice would have their geometrical places in the intricate design, which would be served with cottage cheese, yoghurt and walnuts and a sprinkling of bran or sesame seeds on top. The result resembled a photograph on the cookery page of a glossy magazine – wonderful.

I would frequently be invited to stay and join them and it always seemed a violation to attack the exquisite beauty of Belinda's latest, healthy creation, merely in order to eat it. Wafer-thin slices of hot toast would be covered by a cloth in order to retain the heat. The butter would be in slim, golden curls on an iced dish.

There would be pristine, white napery with sparkling, crystal glasses and shining cutlery – just as Terry liked it. All combined to create an atmosphere more reminiscent of a meal at the Savoy than at a metal table in a Majorcan garden.

In Ibiza, they had been used to not one tiny kitchen, but five large ones. And for most of their married life they had had servants. But now, apart from doing the usual household chores, shopping and answering their correspondence, Belinda had to dress and wash Terry every morning, assist him whenever he went to the lavatory, bath him, administer enemas, give him all his pills at the right time, massage him and change his slippers at two-hourly intervals, in order to air and refresh the ones he had been wearing.

I knew that she had to get up in the middle of the night, sometimes, to attend him. During the periods when he was suffering from a prolonged attack, she would not go to bed at all but would sit up with him all night, watching over him from an armchair.

She looked wan and exhausted, easily became frustrated, but was never conspicuously short-tempered. Consciously, she did her best to create and maintain a tranquil atmosphere in the house at all times, knowing, from past experience, that conflict was bad for Terry's condition. She was delighted to see how compiling the book was bucking-up his spirits by exercising his mind. Many times she provided a name or a film-title when Terry's memory failed him. Or she would give a gentle prompt so that he was able to recount an anecdote in his own way. Throughout, she was extremely helpful to me though she sometimes scolded me when she thought I was working Terry too hard.

Some mornings, on the way to Bonanova, I would have to go via Palma's Olivar market, armed with a large basket, to buy Belinda's shopping requirements which she had listed over the telephone. Often, she only just managed to catch me as I was leaving home.

Other days she would take the opportunity of Terry's being accompanied, to dash out to the shops while I was there. She didn't like to leave him on his own in the cottage. That was when it was my turn to assist him if he needed to 'make a call', as he mock-delicately put it. His own shaking fingers could not manipulate buttons or zips but he refused the alternative of sitting all day with open flies.

'A gentleman,' he said, firmly, 'even one with Parkinson's, doesn't do that.'

Once, Belinda made a request which I'm afraid I turned down.

'Would you like to give Terry a bath tomorrow?' she asked me. 'You are getting on so well together and I'm sure he would love it.'

As I had never bathed anyone, not even a baby, I felt that bathing Terry-Thomas was a little beyond my scope and tactfully declined.

As months went by, Terry's health noticeably deteriorated. Some days he could chat for only a few minutes before apologizing and taking to his bed. Other times he was either too unwell to begin a conversation or having begun, would suddenly lapse into silence and stare aimlessly at the ground.

Yet there were periods when he would brighten and briefly be on top form again. At such times, to give him a change of scene, the three of us would occasionally go out to lunch, after our session ended, Terry nattily dressed for the outing, but with a woolly hat on his head.

I would always have to choose one of the Palma restaurants where the entrance and dining room were on ground level. Steps, either up or down, were difficult for him to manage.

Preliminary planning was called for, because by now he had become such a recluse and felt so shaky and unsure of himself, he did not want to be recognized. If anyone should spot him, he didn't want to know about it.

I was given my instructions about this. I had to telephone (or visit) the restaurant, in advance, to order a table for three, in a quiet corner. Then I would ask for the head waiter and say something like this: 'One of my guests is a very famous man who wishes, at all costs, to remain incognito. Even though he is older now, some members of your staff might recognize him and want to shake his hand. Please restrain them from doing so as this would worry him very much. And should you see any customers approaching our table, please head them off.'

It always worked, but naturally, the staff-warning became a challenge. Who was this famous old man who would be coming in for lunch?

The doorman, the man behind the bar and the waiters would all be very deliberately 'not looking' as Terry shuffled in with Belinda and me. Then an excited whisper would go round when his identity was discovered. He was thus admired from afar but no autographs would be asked for, and this is what Terry wanted because even scribbling his name was now an effort and he certainly did not want to have to chat to strangers. It also, of course, ensured that we always got impeccable service. Perhaps that was the real reason for the elaborate instructions given me.

Terry was on sparkling form the day we went to Palma's smart Club de Mar restaurant. As the waiter carefully placed Belinda's buttered sole before her, he whispered politely, 'Señora.' As Terry's succulent, grilled swordfish was presented, the waiter bowed and smiled, 'Señor.' Then as I received my salmon, the waiter lowered his head and said softly. 'Caballero.'

'Did you understand that, Mack?' cooed Belinda to Terry,

using her pet-name for him. 'He called *you* "Mr" and *Terry* "gentleman".'

For a fraction of a minute there was a flash of the old Terry-Thomas. An eyebrow went up, the top lip slightly curled and with that same caddish inflection one remembered from all those 1950 British comedies he'd been in, Terry aimed a withering glance at the obsequious waiter's departing back and said, loudly, 'Fucking cheek!'

For Belinda and me, it was a magic moment. We fell about and soon Terry was also giggling and looking pleased with himself. Our laughter was applause to him and he relished it. Sadly, moments like that were rare.

Just occasionally he would come out with the odd hilarious quip which would have me genuinely shaking with mirth and momentarily put a stop to the note-taking. 'That's a marvellous one. That definitely goes in,' I would say. Once again Terry would chuckle and look cockily triumphant.

But I was careful not to overdo it. He would have seen through forced laughter and he wouldn't have liked that at all.

Always the gentleman, he was ever apologizing when Parkinson's prevented him from getting out the story he wanted to tell. He might forget the punchline or simply be unable to get his tongue round a crucial word like plethora. Then he would get cross with himself: 'Dammit! I've been telling that since I was five, and now I muck it up.'

Early on in our talks he struggled one day for nearly half an hour, determined to explain something a bit complicated (the *Private Eye* libel case) which just would not come out right. Eventually, he gave up and said, sombrely, 'Thank you for your tolerance. This Parkinson's is a bugger, isn't it? How come you are able to be so patient with me? Why is it?'

I reminded him that my mother, Dorothy Blandford, who had died a few months before, in a Portsmouth old people's home, had also suffered from Parkinson's Disease.

This news seemed to please him. 'Ah, of course,' he said. 'I knew I'd chosen the right chap. That's why this book's working out.'

What I didn't tell him was that there were often heart-turning moments for me when Parkinson's produced a certain vulnerable expression on his face, or a familiar sequence of arm-jerking, which caused me to 'see' (with very little imagination) not Terry-Thomas sitting there, huddled in a dressing gown, but my mother.

As we neared the end of the book, it became more and more difficult for him to recall anecdotes and certainly not funny ones. Trying to jog his memory, one day, I began to go through a list of stars with whom I knew he had worked but who had not yet been mentioned.

'You once made a film with Joan Crawford, Terry. What was she like?'

'All right,' came the reply.

'Is that all? Isn't there anything more you can recall about JOAN CRAWFORD, of all people?'

'No.'

'Oh! Well, what about Shelley Winters, then?'

'Fat!'

'Oh, come on Terry. Nothing we can say about Shelley that's more complimentary than that?'

'No, sorry.'

'I bet you can do better with Debbie Reynolds. Do you remember making *How Sweet It Is* with her, in 1968?'

'Yes. Silly film.'

'And Debbie?'

'I believe she was Jewish.'

'Apart from her religion...' I began.

'LOOK. I don't think your list is going to work. I never liked lists,' said Terry, tartly. 'Sorry, but I'm feeling lousy. Do you mind if we stop for today?'

In all fairness, it was not often that Terry curtailed our sessions like that, not unless he was really suffering or couldn't concentrate. Professional right to the end, he knew we still needed more good material, and battled on bravely, trying to winkle amusing incidents from obscure recesses in his mind.

'This book is going to be my last fling – my final performance! It's got to be really funny; people will expect that,' Terry reprimanded himself, one morning. 'Believe me, I've been trying so hard all night to come up with something risible that'll please us. I must have a million "goodies" tucked away in my head. But they won't come out.'

The first draft of *Terry-Thomas Tells Tales* was completed by Easter 1984. Then began what Terry had always maintained he was looking forward to: the arduous task of revising. By now he could not concentrate on reading anything for long – even about himself – so I had to read out the whole book to him, making corrections as we went. It took weeks and many changes were made. Things were deleted or rearranged, other sequences extended and some suspended 'on hold'.

When we reached the end, I retyped and began again, this time to read the rewritten version out loud to him. Several weeks (and many more changes) later, when we had completed that, I typed it out once more and we repeated the process. And so it went on, but each time the corrections were fewer. Seven times we went over the MS in this way and, on the last reading, the blue pencil was hardly used. At last it was time to send Terry's book off to a publisher. It was now late summer 1984.

But Terry was reluctant to let the MS go. 'I know I've not been as hilarious as I ought to have been,' he worried. 'Leave it with me. I'm going to go over it by myself and try to bung in a few more funny bits. People who buy books by comedians want value for their money.'

At first, when I periodically called in to check on progress, the MS would be open, beside Terry's chair. But usually, he had made scant alterations and no humorous injections at all.

To read for more than a couple of minutes eventually became impossible for him. He would have to put the MS aside and rest. Then he might not feel up to attempting to resume for days. Or a whole week. Or even months. It was very frustrating to realize that a year had gone by since we had last gone over it together. Yet eager though he was to see his book in print, he pushed away my pleas to allow me to send off the MS as it stood.

'I'm convinced that tomorrow, some more funny bits will occur to me. Positive!' he whispered, in a voice I could hardly hear. 'I'm really sorry about all this delay, Terry; it must be sickening for you. But this book will be my epitaph. It'll still be here after I've gone. And I do want to be remembered as a *comedian.*'

That was the last time I ever heard him speak. On my subsequent visits to Bonanova he had given up talking. He would be sitting in a chair staring blankly into space. Chin resting on his chest, he would nod weakly at my greeting. The MS would always be near by, but not often open. He would jerkily move his desperate gaze towards it and attempt a feeble, apologetic smile. He had become thin, hollow-eyed and shrunken.

Belinda, looking considerably older now, and so careworn, tried to reassure me that on good days he still picked up a pencil and made vain efforts to get on with the task. I could tell she was just being kind.

When Terry and Belinda left Majorca a couple of years ago, for London, he had still only reached page 90 of the 250-page MS.

By now their funds had got so low they were reduced to living on hand-outs. An exclusive *Daily Mirror* story, on 9 December 1988, revealed that they were living in a church-charity flat in south-west London. The Entertainment Artistes' Benevolent Fund had provided bedding, furniture, carpets and a £2,000 electrically operated bed.

An appeal was subsequently launched and brought in £5,000 from *Daily Mirror* readers. Another £5,000 was contributed by television viewers. A disturbing TV programme about Terry had shown just how wretched the one-time, debonair cad-about-town, once a millionaire but now living in poverty, had become.

Four months later, an all-star charity show for him, at

London's Theatre Royal, raised £75,000. Terry was too ill to attend but saw the show on video. And cried.

On 11 August 1989, readers of Nigel Dempster's column in the *Daily Mail* learned that Terry had been moved into a £200-a-week nursing home in Surrey and had so improved under specialist treatment that he was speaking again.

Terry's death was announced on the 1 o'clock news on 8 January 1990, after a nurse had found him dead in bed. His painful struggles were over.

Belinda was informed of his demise in the clinic where she was said to be recovering from a nervous breakdown, having been admitted a few days before.

At Terry's funeral, on 17 January, the props which had helped to catapult him to stardom were there. Resting on a heart-shaped lace cushion at the head of the procession were his monocle, a cigarette holder and a clove carnation; the only missing trademark was one of his fancy waistcoats. The theme from *Those Magnificent Men in Their Flying Machines* was played at the service.

Among the numerous show business mourners, Terry would perhaps have been most gratified to know that Eric Sykes had come to say farewell. They had first worked together, in 1958, in *Large as Life*, which Terry described in his book as 'my favourite time at the Palladium'. Later Eric had played his man in *Magnificent Men* and *Monte Carlo or Bust* and, of course, most recently they had hilariously appeared in that famous world prize-winning tobacco commercial set in a London underground station.

After that, while Terry was eager, and despite pressing offers from the advertising agency, they had never worked together again. Terry had always been puzzled, and quite hurt, as to why Eric had not wanted to continue the winning combination. 'I wonder whatever I did to upset him,' he pondered many times. 'We were the greatest of pals.'

That Eric had travelled to Godalming, Surrey, to be at his funeral, would surely have pleased him.

Although *Terry-Thomas Tells Tales* never achieved

perfectionist Terry's criterion, because he had been intent on making it even funnier, I felt that as a tribute to him, the book should be published as he last left it.

It was, after all, the longest 'interview' he had ever given. His 'final performance', as he described it, deserved to go on record.

Some years have elapsed since he dictated it to me in that sunny, Majorcan garden, beneath the waving palm fronds. But I have not updated it. These were Terry's tales, as he told them....

Terry Daum, Palma, Majorca
1990

Filmography

Terry-Thomas's many films include:
The Brass Monkey 1948
Helter Skelter 1948
Date with a Dream
Melody Club
The Queen Walks
Private's Progress 1956
The Green Man 1956
Brothers in Law 1957
Happy Is the Bride 1957
Blue Murder at St Trinian's 1957
The Naked Truth 1957
Lucky Jim 1957
Tom Thumb 1958
Carleton Browne of the F.O 1958
I'm All Right Jack 1959
Too Many Crooks 1959
School for Scoundrels 1960
Make Mine Mink 1960
His and Hers 1960
A Matter of Who 1961
Operation Snatch 1961
Bachelor Flat 1961
The Wonderful World of the Brothers Grimm 1962

Kill or Cure 1962
The Mouse on the Moon 1963
The Wild Affair 1963
It's a Mad Mad Mad Mad World 1963
How to Murder Your Wife 1964
Those Magnificent Men in Their Flying Machines 1965
Paradise 1965
Easy Come Easy Go 1965
You Must Be Joking 1965
Munster Go Home 1966
Strange Bedfellows 1966
Kiss the Girls and Make Them Die 1966
The Sandwich Man 1966
Our Man in Marrakesh 1966
2000 Years Later 1966
Top Crack 1966
Jules Verne's Rocket to the Moon 1967
Don't Look Now We're Being Shot At (La Grande Vadrouille) 1967
A Guide for the Married Man 1967
Don't Raise the Bridge, Lower the River 1967
Dorrelik 1967
Pig Malione 1967
Diabolik 1967
The Perils of Pauline 1967
The Karate Killers 1967
How Sweet It Is 1968
Arabella 1968
Where Were You When the Lights Went Out 1968
Monte Carlo or Bust 1968
Seven Times Seven 1969
Thirteen 1969
Atlantic Wall 1970
The Abominable Dr Phibes 1970
Arthur Arthur 1970
Golpo Grosso grossissimo anzi Probabile 1971
Dr Phibes Rises Again 1971

Lei, Lui, Loro, la Legge 1971
The Cherry Picker 1972
Robin Hood 1973
Vault of Horror 1973
The Heroes 1974
Tradition 1974
Spanish Fly 1975
The Last Remake of Beau Geste 1976
The Bawdy Adventures of Tom Jones 1976
Side by Side 1976
The Hound of the Baskervilles 1978
House of Dr Coppelia 1978
Uno Scacco Tutto Matto
Checkmate For McDowell
How to Kill 400 Duponts